In the future days, which we seek to make secure, we look forward to a world founded upon four essential human freedoms.

The first is freedom of speech and expression—everywhere in the world.

The second is freedom of every person to worship God in his own way—everywhere in the world.

The third is freedom from want, which, translated into world terms, means economic understandings which will secure to every nation a healthy peacetime life for its inhabitants—everywhere in the world.

The fourth is freedom from fear, which, translated into world terms, means a worldwide reduction of armaments to such a point and in such a thorough fashion that no nation will be in a position to commit an act of physical aggression against any neighbour—anywhere in the world.

That is no vision of a distant millennium. It is a definite basis for a kind of world attainable in our own time and generation…

Freedom means the supremacy of human rights everywhere. Our support goes to those who struggle to gain those rights and keep them. Our strength is our unity of purpose.

To that high concept there can be no end save victory.

Franklin Delano Roosevelt

David W. Shannon B.A., LL.B., LL.M.

Six Degrees of Dignity:
Disability in an Age of Freedom

 Published by Creative Bound International Inc.
1-800-287-8610
www.creativebound.com

ISBN 978-1-894439-31-2
Printed and bound in Canada
Copyright © 2007 David W. Shannon

Production by Creative Bound International Inc.
Managing editor Gail Baird
Creative director Wendelina O'Keefe
Text editor Ruth Bradley-St-Cyr
Cover photos by Brad Stephenson – Superior Filmworks

Library and Archives Canada Cataloguing in Publication

Shannon, David W., 1963-
        Six degrees of dignity : disability in an age of freedom / David
W. Shannon.

Includes bibliographical references.
ISBN 978-1-894439-31-2

        1. People with disabilities—Canada. 2. Equality—Canada.
3. Dignity. I. Title.
HV1559.C3S48 2006   305.9'080971   C2006-906069-X

To all the persons with a disability and
their loved ones who daily, quietly educate
the world on why it will be so much
better when all people belong equally.
They can trust that their voices
join to create an orchestral
performance heard by a Nation.

Acknowledgements

AT A TIME that falls upon the heels of devastating cuts to disability programs in the nineties, an era of broad post 9/11 control, and the Harper Government's recent decision to cut the Charter Challenges program, it seems important to acknowledge and thank all members of civil society who continue to fight for human rights and fundamental freedoms.

The individuals and organizations that have been devoted to the promotion of disability rights must be recognized as personal role models, and thanked for the work they have done to ensure the creation of a rights culture in Canada. These leaders include Henry Enns, Alan Simpson, Marcia Rioux, Bengt Lindquist, Maxine Tynes, David Baker, Catherine Frazee, Traci Walters, Paul-Claude Bérubé, Laurie Beachell, Sam Sullivan, Ron Ross, and Dave Koivisto. They and so many others have helped advance a social movement that has been an inspiration, education, and benefit to so many million Canadians and people worldwide. As a result of their passionate work, should persons with a disability face a challenge to the preservation of their rights, it is a setback rather than a reversal of time to a period where charity, fear, and benevolent institutionalization ruled their lives.

My many friends at the Canadian Association of Independent Living Centres, Council of Canadians with Disabilities, Handicapped Action Group Thunder Bay, Tetra Society of North America, Disability Rights Promotion International, and Disabled Persons International must also be congratulated for delivering the organizational capacity that brings connectedness to what is now two generations of individual efforts to advance disability rights.

My former spouse, Alison Denton, must be acknowledged and thanked for urging me to undertake this project. Although our marriage was dissolving throughout much of the period of this writing, she remained encouraging, and that is truly appreciated.

Lisa Campbell, thank you for your elegant dare at the inception of this writing and your continued input. Further thanks must be given to Steven Estey, Katherine Guernsey, Irmo Marini, Anny Jolimore, Dave Baxter, Joanne Peach, Luke de Sadeleer, Troy Myers, and Anna Marie Sarto for their contributions, support and comments. Gail Baird, Wendy O'Keefe, and Ruth St. Cyr at Creative Bound International, your expertise and gentility has been a true joy in the completion of this project. Family support, as always, has meant so much in the progress of this text. My team in that mighty tiny law office we all too often call home—Leon Bullock, Tammy Lehtinen, June Bjorn, and Mark Lucas—your talents and ability to dedicate each working day to the protection of rights is truly appreciated.

Suzanne Boudreau, thank you for your inspiration, honesty and poetry as this text is lifted to the reading public. Your sensitivity and support continues to show me the creative with mastery and magnificence.

Glossary

ADA	Americans with a Disability Act
AODA	Accessibility for Ontarians with Disabilities Act
ASAC	Accessibility Standards Advisory Council
BFJ	Bona fide justification
BFOR	Bona fide occupational requirement
CAILC	Canadian Association of Independent Living Centres
CCD	Council of Canadians with Disabilities
FCA	Federal Court of Appeal
IL	Independent Living
NGO	Non-Governmental Organization
ODA	Ontarians with Disabilities Act
PWD	Person with a Disability
UNCRDPWD	UN Convention of the Rights and Dignity of Persons With a Disability

Contents

Introduction

*In the fight for freedom which puts its stamp so strongly on present-day life,
the final issue is what dignity we are willing to give to man.*

Dag Hammarskjold, from address at
Johns Hopkins University, June 14, 1955

I HAVE NEVER MET ANYONE who has deliberately discriminated against persons with a disability. I have met many people who unwittingly marginalized, denied choice, or caused an individual with a disability to be isolated. I have met even more persons with disabilities who have scratched for dignity, for an assertion of the self, and tried to find decent opportunities in an indecent situation.

Even today, it is all too common to attempt to enter a restaurant, special event, or even the front doors of the Canadian Parliament buildings only to find that there is no ramp to make it accessible to persons in a wheelchair. For some reason, this is considered acceptable. If there was a sign in front of any of these facilities that proclaimed "no Jews," "no coloured persons," or "no women" were allowed, there would be unprecedented revolt. However, this happens daily to persons with a disability when they attempt to be mobile within Canadian society. There appears to be both a problem of historical happenstance and normalized perspective. One perspective is that in terms of civil rights movements, persons with a disability are simply the latest in a long line of special interest groups, asserting integration into the mainstream. Racism may have been acceptable in some sectors fifty years ago, but we would be appalled to hear racist slurs in public today. Able-ist actions and slogans simply need another fifty years to be on a par with such reprehensible behaviour.

There is also a bizarre twist at the source of these forms of discrimination. Whereas racism, sexism, and religious bigotry often arise from hatred, able-ism is typically rooted in pity or fear. The discriminator pities the poor disabled person for his or her wretched existence, or fears that such a hideous reality could be visited upon them. These contrasting roots may have much to do with the ability to combat the discrimination because the former is so blatant and the latter so insidious. However, there may also be the ugly underbelly of society articulated by the character of Cartman in the often-humorous, satirical animated series *South Park*, where he suggests that the disabled were simply put on this earth for his amusement.

The purpose of this book is to discuss equality and the promotion of dignity for persons with a disability today. It is not an exercise in cataloguing problems and barriers, which indeed would be a boring diversion, providing only minimal catharsis, and is a job best left to an overwrought policy nerd or rabid disability separatist. I prefer to build a constructive thesis that outlines goals for working toward true dignity. Inequality for persons with a disability has everything to do with the denial of dignity, and that dignity cannot be reclaimed without several supports in place to promote inclusion. What dignity is and how it is obtained will be the thrust of this discussion.

Canadian society is founded on a classical liberal understanding of the self. This perspective regards human dignity as the primary social and personal value. Dignity is realized through an individual freedom that is manifested in meaningful decision making and exercise of individual responsibility. On this basis, the self is regarded as an autonomous, self-determining entity worthy of recognition and respect from others.

The right to dignity for all is explicitly recognized in Canadian law. In practice, however, socio-economic and historical circumstance has conspired to debar a variety of individuals and groups from the concern and respect their nature as persons demands. Prominent among these excluded groups are members of the disabled community who, for reasons to be examined, are marginalized by a society that regularly neglects to recognize their needs, capacities, and merits as individuals.

Dignity for persons with disabilities must be pursued as a meaningful goal that enhances society in general, not just the lives of persons with a disability (PWDs). Building on current social norms and legal interpretations of rights for the disabled, this book will identify some of the social and attitudinal barriers still present in Canadian society. Six factors are needed to reverse social and attitudinal exclusion. These are:

1. Dignity in Public Perception
2. Dignity in the Community
3. Dignity in Law
4. Dignity in Public Policy
5. Dignity of Self
6. Dignity in Future

Each component must work in concert to, in essence, create a symphony of dignity—a crescendo of equality that contrasts the current dissonance in both theory and practice that perpetuates the marginalization of individuals in the disability community.

Each degree of dignity forms a chapter in the discussion. The hope is that by the end of the book the thematic threads will tie together to form a concrete plan for advancing society towards true inclusion.

Dignity in Public Perception

Perception of persons with a disability is a complicated process with its own dynamic and history. There are several interconnected and overlapping perceptions that serve to define PWDs in the public arena. A common thread of this history is found to lie in a systematic denial of free choice and the imposition of physical and psychological constraints incompatible with their dignity as persons. Prior transformations in public perception point the way towards the possibility of further changes leading to a more positive awareness of the disabled and their requirement of dignity.

The negative impact of stereotypical images of disability currently portrayed in mass media and in popular art forms harms both public perception and the individual's sense of dignity. Broad communication strategies targeted at reversing these discriminatory portrayals are clearly needed. As well, PWDs are vastly over-represented in our criminal justice system due to our outdated perceptions of "deviance."

Dignity in the Community

For many individuals with disabilities, the family and local community constitute the principal places of interaction with others. These local spaces tend to be more "informal" than mainstream society, being organized around sets of norms and values that have evolved to suit particular circumstance. While this sometimes enables greater dignity and respect, it is also true that it may enjoin increased dependence and internalization of subordination.

It is critical to address this problem by suggesting practical alternatives in the area of personal care and housing. In particular, an examination of the positive impact of the "Independent Living Movement," community living movement or deinstitutionalization, all of which seek to maximize autonomy for persons with disabilities in an environment where their own needs are self-directed and barrier-free. As well, employment issues need to be addressed in a way that enhances opportunities for PWDs to contribute their skills and benefit from economic participation.

Dignity in Law

There has been progressive judicial decision making to assist persons with disabilities in achieving equality. Key among these advances has been the evolution of the legal duty to accommodate, but this should be seen as a first step rather than as an end in itself.

The promotion and protection of individual dignity is anchored in Section 15, the equality provision of the Canadian Charter of Rights and Freedoms. "Equality" itself is an exceptionally broad concept that is not easy to define and is, indeed, frequently interpreted in a variety of mutually incongruent ways; however, it is explicitly identified in terms of autonomy and self-determination. The interplay of the needs of persons with a disability and the purpose of the Charter will be discussed more fully, highlighting how the judiciary in Canada has provided a cornerstone for the protection of disability rights.

Dignity in Public Policy

Government funding cuts have had an adverse impact upon potentially innovative policy changes toward the betterment of the lives and promotion of independence for PWDs. This reality is juxtaposed against governmental assertions since 1981, the UN International Year of Persons with a Disability, that its policies and programs are achieving dignity and autonomy for PWDs. We will examine the purpose and effectiveness of the series of policy initiatives that in recent years have been introduced to address the needs of the disabled, and determine improvements that must be undertaken. The Accessibility for Ontarians with a Disability Act (AODA) illustrates both the opportunity and barriers to developing effective policy.

Dignity of Self

Rational decision making, freedom of choice, self-respect, physical and psychological integrity, and personal empowerment are integral to all persons. To achieve this, many social and economic barriers to the construction of an authentic self must be removed as well as analyzing how forms of internalized subordination have been imposed on the disabled by others. Through empowerment and overcoming alienation and exclusion, the dignity of the disabled self can be reclaimed. Persons with a disability are faced with a paradox: while society has created and maintained barriers that result in isolation, essential social relationships require pain, excitement, and risk. Is it better to be safe and cloistered by the paternalism that drives discrimination of the disabled, or does one wish to risk the gains and losses inherent in romantic, filial, and familial relationships?

Dignity in Future

Building on the analysis and conclusions of the previous five degrees, a further necessary point to promoting equality for PWDs is to establish a major forward-looking goal in order to create a broad, common consensus and hope for PWDs. The objective is to propose a practical model of legal initiative, social change, policy initiative, and attitudinal transition. By means of this model, current states of exclusion and subordination can be transcended and autonomy and self-determination restored to the disabled.

The International Year of Disabled Persons, 1981, brought mixed results in Canada, but now, 25 years later, the United Nations is working on a bold, new step—the Convention on the Rights and Dignity of Persons with a Disability currently being negotiated by all member states. This international human rights treaty combines the protection of individual and group rights while creating a framework for positive policy and public perception changes. Furthermore, the implementation of the Convention will be monitored and greater enforcement will be assured through negotiation of a quasi-judicial body that can receive individual complaints for a breach of any article of the convention. This chapter will consider progress made to date in negotiating this treaty, and its potential for benefiting the 600 million PWDs worldwide.

Conclusion

Six Degrees of Dignity is the program for a new way of thinking and acting. Dignity and autonomy for people with disabilities must be promoted in a holistic way that has all Canadians truly believing in the benefits that our society and culture can gain by including PWDs in a meaningful way. We all must embrace the notion that our culture will advance when persons with a disability no longer face unnecessary barriers to living more wide-ranging and substantial lives.

CHAPTER 1

A Personal Journey Toward Dignity

" The now-too-familiar whine of the motors cut into the internalized cold—I don't think that it was audible, but it moved from feet to ankles, knees, hips, groin, chest, nipples, face, jaw—an electric never-ending jolt upwards, like a spinal cord injury in reverse. What day was it? Day 4? Day 6? Day 11? I had already lost track, but it was not a score. It was just the need to move forward, while being enveloped by what was behind.

Undulation—with whispering flickering golden grass defying winter cold, as it grasped for summer sun—this was the nature of the road. Over, blue sky, down, shade, shadow, up, painted bright brilliant blue, red, yellow houses—then over, down—smell of ocean and cold, whine, hum, move up down—break! Brilliant. Crescent of ocean, shimmering light that reaches its tentacles to my chest pulling human and spirit forward in union, a cathartic spiritual elevation found in the ending of goal achievement, and the beginning of next, which was the splintering of physicality and the equality of the real. The immersion of nature, the ancient, the future, the frost, the warmth, the every laugh and cry, the elevation of being where disability was beyond environmental limitation and immersed in the ever-present universal flow.

I had made it to the other side of Newfoundland! "

∽

THE SIX DEGREES OF DIGNITY can be seen as an achievable end that is so very close for persons with disabilities and, indeed, all Canadians. It is extrinsically near, and is also a metaphor for intrinsic advancement. In effect, it is a journey.

A journey is often defined by its objectives. The journey that I want to tell you about began 25 years ago with an injury to my spinal cord, and it is both a personal and physical one. I simply wish to give you a little background in order to illustrate that most of my critique and argument throughout this discussion arises from lived experiences, with skills in legal and public advocacy being used as a response to discrimination, as if they were tools pulled from a shed.

"Wheelchairs Freak Me Out"

In my final year of high school one of my passions was rugby. I was selected for the Nova Scotia junior rugby team, and represented the province at the 1981 Canada Games. I was also heavily involved in the drama club and participated on the student council.

The next semester I enrolled at the University of Waterloo, and joined the university rugby team as a way to meet people and make friends. That proved to be a life-altering act. On September 23, 1981, two weeks into my new life at university, I was on the field practising with my teammates. They were in a scrum. The scrum collapsed—with me on the bottom. The play moved on. I did not.

It was surreal. I was wide awake and remember everything. Emotionally and intellectually, I was moving with the play. Physically, I lay where I had fallen. It was an utter perversion of reality. Intellectually, I knew what was going on, but emotionally, I did not. In the ambulance on the way to the hospital, I asked the coach, "Is this permanent?" He didn't know what to say.

Ironically, the United Nations General Assembly had proclaimed 1981 the International Year of Disabled Persons, to "promote 'equality' and 'full participation' of disabled persons in social life and development."[1] I remember trying to tune out the nearly continuous radio ads and bulletins about disability

1. For more information on the International Year of Disabled Persons visit: http://www.unac.org/en/news_events/zun_days/disabled1.asp.

and breaking down barriers that seemed to intrude upon us from all sides that summer. I told my best friend, Troy, "I don't care what they say. Wheelchairs freak me out."

Within sixty days of making that remark, I was flat on my back on a Stryker bed. Even when I heard the diagnosis—that my neck had been broken at the cervical 4–5 level and the likelihood of ever walking again was nil—I thought, "Oh yeah, I'll just pick up and go on." I was in denial for a very long time. Of course, I was only 18 years old.

When news of my injury reached Nova Scotia, five of my high school friends immediately flew to Waterloo. They spent two weeks, day in and day out, at my side. The support I felt was overwhelming. Friends continued to come from Nova Scotia to visit. They came during the Christmas holidays and again during the February break. Although I could no longer walk, there was never a sense that our socializing would change. That truly helped me.

Life was, on one level, completely different—yet on another, strangely the same. I could no longer walk and required help with many things that had never been an issue before my injury. I used a wheelchair to get around, and my days of playing rugby were definitely over. However, my desire to jump with both feet into whatever life had to offer remained undiminished.

Once my injury was stabilized, I was transferred from the hospital in Kitchener, Ontario, to the Lyndhurst Rehabilitation Centre in Toronto, and was finally discharged in April 1982. With the support of good friends and family, the desire to reassert my independence, and an opportunity to return to school, I took up the fight against prejudice and discrimination to prove to myself and the broader world that I was still a normal person. My friends hadn't bought into the perception that I was different now. Their support affirmed that I was the same person I had been on that September day before rugby practice.

The support that I was given was surely critical to getting back on track. Ironically, although those closest to me did not perceive our relationship as being different, as I re-entered the community, I was overwhelmed by how diminished the expectations of others were simply because I now used a wheelchair. Nonetheless, I went back to school, and completed my undergraduate studies at Lakehead University in Thunder Bay and my law degree at Dalhousie University in Halifax. My graduate law studies were at the London School of Economics and Political Science.

It was during law school that I began to find myself, in an academic (as opposed to personal) fashion, wanting to further investigate what causes the barriers between the individual with disabilities and the community; in other words, what inhibits their full inclusion and personal expression in the community. Although while in London the opportunity to frequent pubs and tapas bars and take the occasional bungee jump did avail itself, it was a great place to begin deeper studies into how difference becomes discrimination.

Dave Shannon's Cross Canada Tour

In 1997, as a way to promote the potential of all persons with a disability, I journeyed across Canada in my wheelchair. Dave Shannon's Cross Canada Tour began on April 1, 1997, in Cape Speare, Newfoundland, and ended in Stanley Park in Vancouver, British Columbia, on October 10, 1997. The trip took me within 25 kilometres of 90 percent of the Canadian population. I went more than 9,000 kilometres—5,400 miles—over a span of 197 days.

The goals of the tour were inspired by Martin Luther King Junior's "I Have a Dream" speech: "I have a dream that my four little children will one day live in a nation where they will not be judged by the color of their skin, but the content of their character." It is also my dream that one day no person will be judged by physical characteristics, whether they be gender, skin colour, physical disability, or any other. With a truly extraordinary support team, and hundreds of volunteers from our national sponsor, the Bank of Nova Scotia, we promoted greater community inclusion and advancement of persons with a disability with every kilometre. We also demonstrated that teamwork, partnerships and community inclusion are the best aspects of Canadian society, and its national identity.

The cross-Canada tour was a physical journey, and also a metaphor for the potential of persons with disability: that denial of dignity and equality is primarily a matter of perception, not a tangible concept with merit. The value of an individual should be measured by the existence of one's spirit, not the difference of one's physicality.

It was also a personal journey. It was an attempt to regain something that had been lost. Since my spinal cord injury in 1981, several of my activities, and much public perception towards me, had been defined by loss: loss of ability, loss of mobility, loss of capability, and loss of potentiality. Therefore, in addition to promoting public awareness, by crossing Canada, I hoped that I could dispel those myths surrounding me as a person and in so doing reclaim what seemed to have disappeared.

When a group is marginalized or discriminated against, a net economic, social, and cultural loss occurs for the entire community. A statement that captures this sense of loss to both the marginalized group and the community as a whole is from the latter scenes of the movie *Blade Runner*. The human replicant, just prior to his death, gives a poignant reflection on his life, which would end unfulfilled and had been marred by constant marginalization. By definition he was an outsider, but said: "I've seen things you people wouldn't believe. Attack ships on fire off the shoulder of Orion. Watched sea beams glitter in the dark near tenhouse gate. All those moments will be lost, like tears in the rain."

At the end of the cross-Canada journey, I felt as though I too had the pleasure of seeing sea beams…only they were truly from Canadian natural beauty; star-filled nights over the prairies, filtering sunlight fairy-like as it bounced from the powerful, sometimes menacing depths of the Atlantic Ocean, forests gripping the road as if to envelop all passersby, and the Rockies jetting seemingly endlessly skyward, threaded by monstrous canyons and gorge boundaries. I had seen all this. It was uppermost in my psyche, and was now integral to my identity, but with the physical journey now over I was troubled by the questions: What had changed for the betterment of persons with a disability? Had awareness of the inherent dignity and potential for equality of disabled persons been increased?

The cross-Canada tour had reached over one million people through public appearances and the media. I had the pleasure of working with a volunteer base that numbered in the thousands, but like the replicant in *Blade Runner*, I was left at the end of this journey with a sense of unfulfillment as I considered these questions. However, arising from this doubt was a monumental sense that no one and nothing could take away my memories, and the knowledge that the goal of threading across Canada at 11 kilometres per hour had been achieved.

Outcomes of the Tour

There were several positive outcomes of the cross-Canada tour:

- We demonstrated a model of public, private and non-profit partnerships that promote public awareness and education of disability issues.
- We exemplified the potential for building communities and empowering people with a disability through a combined effort of several sectors of the Canadian community.
- We showed that a national project can be directed from a relatively small city, in this case Thunder Bay, Ontario.

As a person with quadriplegia, I had several personal care needs. Notwithstanding these potentially large barriers, the fact that I crossed Canada with the support of an excellent road team showed that people, whatever their station, can overcome obstacles with support.

Tour facts

»	Kilometres traveled:	9,000
»	Number of days to complete tour	197
»	Number of wheeling days	120
»	Time in pre-tour planning	2 years
»	Number of volunteers and participants	5,000
»	Number of staff	5
»	Number of road team members	3
»	Number of cars that passed by on the road	1,440,000
»	Number of people spoken to directly	20,000
»	Length of wheeling day	10 hours
»	Distance travelled on wheeling days	75 km
»	Top speed of wheelchair	11 km/hr
»	Number of wheelchair tires used	12
»	Number of wheelchair motor repairs	3
»	Number of broken ribs (rolled into a ditch near Cobourg, Ontario)	4

After the cross-Canada tour, I looked forward to practising law and bringing to it the knowledge gained during the tour. I was also determined that my work be inspired with the same questions and objectives that motivated the trip: Can law raise an individual's dignity rather than merely compensate a loss? Can law empower the disadvantaged, rather than be used as a tool that disempowers the needy? In effect, the journey took on an intellectual and sometimes strategic, pragmatic turn.

The next step in the journey was to address the protection and promotion of human rights. In addition to practising law, I have been a member of the Ontario Human Rights Tribunal, and continue to work in several other volunteer capacities. This journey was also about understanding that discrimination can occur when we pretend a disability is not present and call it equality.

Equality can be achieved and dignity restored by acknowledging apparent physical differences, and accommodating needs as they arise. For example, an employer can help a valued employee who has a disability realize his or her potential by instituting appropriate supports. When that inclusion occurs, the whole community benefits in subtle, overt, and profound ways because it benefits from *all* of its citizens. It is a wonderful goal, the goal of inclusion, the celebration of diversity, and it is an amazing collective journey when this goal is pursued together. In the words of Robert Kennedy: "Each time a man stands up for an ideal, or acts to improve the lot of others, or strikes out against injustice, he sends forth a tiny ripple of hope."

This intellectual and professional journey has brought me to conclude that rights of persons with disabilities will be achieved when economic, social, and cultural rights are realized in a meaningful way by persons with a disability. The value of an individual should be measured by the existence of their spirit, not the difference of his or her physicality.

～

Right: Another Canadian kid with new skates and a hockey stick for Christmas. I couldn't wait to get outside before trying them out!

Above: Coming off the field at halftime during the 1981 Canada Games.

Left: The end of the game. We played well, but I think Ontario trounced us in the end!

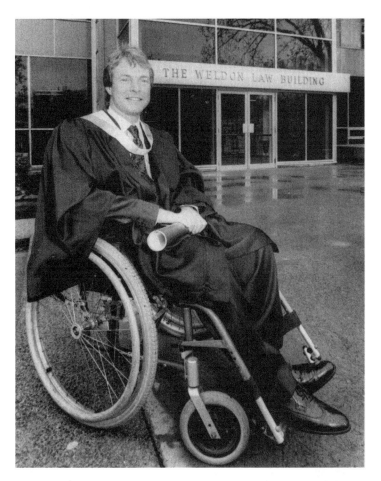

Above: What a day! What a learning experience! Law school convocation.

Right: Being called to the Bar and becoming a member of the Law Society of Upper Canada in 1996 has been a wonderful way to observe first-hand how Canadians see their national identity rooted in the protection of rights.

Arriving in Thunder Bay while wheeling across Canada in 1997, I was able to celebrate with a welcoming crowd in the shadow of one of the greatest—Terry Fox.

Finishing the Cross Canada Tour in October 1997 at Stanley Park, Vancouver. We were all pretty tired—with me, from left to right, are Alison Denton, Rachael Harris and Scott Parker.

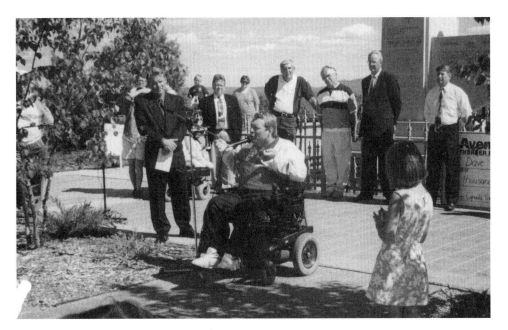

Addressing the welcoming group at the Terry Fox monument in Thunder Bay, July 1997.

Thanks to our tour sponsor Scotiabank, events such as this one in Sydney, Nova Scotia, in May 1997, were held across Canada.

CHAPTER 2

Finding Dignity

Yo', Whatever happened to the values of humanity
Whatever happened to the fairness in equality
Instead in spreading love we spreading animosity
Lack of understanding, leading us away from unity

"Where Is the Love?" from the album *Elephunk*
by the Black Eyed Peas
Lyrics by: will. i. am, Taboo, Apl. de. ap., Justin Timberlake, Ron Fair,
P. Board, G. Pajon Jr., M. Fratantuno, J. Curtis

ACCORDING TO PROVISIONS of Human Rights Codes in Canadian juris-
dictions, preservation of personal dignity is central to the promotion and
maintenance of freedom and equality for Canadian citizens. It is through the
exercise of freedom and equality that individuals are enabled to create themselves as autonomous citizens able to participate as full members of society.
While Canada has done much in past years to promote itself as a nation toler-
ant of diversity, many individuals and groups still remain effectively excluded
by their "differences" from the opportunities and prospects enjoyed by mainstream society. Nowhere is this more evident than in the circumstances and
conditions of Canada's disabled community.

According to a recent Government of Canada report, one in eight
Canadians has a disability (3.6 million people). For Canada's Aboriginal population, the rate of disability is more than one and a half times the rate for the

non-Aboriginal population. Women are more likely than men to have a disability, regardless of age. The most cited forms of disability are mobility related (2.5 million) with the balance affecting hearing, vision, or learning. The number of disabilities and their severity generally increase with age, with a higher proportion of women experiencing more acute levels of disability and accompanying poverty.

There were further findings, as well:

- In 2002, employment rates were only 53% for people with disabilities, compared to 76% for people without;
- Aboriginal adults with disabilities are almost twice as likely to be out of the workforce as Aboriginal adults without disabilities;
- Many working-age adults with disabilities who are unemployed or out of the workforce have the potential to work if they have access to the necessary supports;
- Among working-age adults, those with disabilities are three to four times more likely to have government transfers as their main source of personal income than those without disabilities. But the percentage of those with disabilities citing transfers as their main source of income fell by 5% from 1999 to 2002;
- Aboriginal people, low-income families of children with disabilities, adults with severe disabilities and those living in small or rural communities face added income difficulties.[2]

These figures provide a preliminary indication of the magnitude of the social and economic predicament confronting the disabled community. Yet this is only part of the story. Statistics do not reveal the emotional and financial effect that the disabled have on the lives of millions of other family members, loved ones, neighbours, and co-workers. More significantly, they do not reveal the innumerable difficulties, obstructions, aggravations, and frustrations that each disabled person faces in the detailed course of everyday life: manageable transportation, available housing, accessible educational opportunities, attention to personal needs and admission to leisure and entertainment facilities, to name just a few.

---

2. *Advancing the Inclusion of Persons with Disabilities 2004*, Government of Canada, The Ministry of Human Resources and Social Development Canada, available on the Office for Disability Issues website: http://www.sdc.gc.ca/en/gateways/topics/pyp-pup.shtml.

Using Ontario as an example, beyond the broad socio-cultural contributions that an actualized disability community could make to Ontario, it has been estimated that the potential spending power of Canadians with disabilities is as much as 20 to 25 billion dollars. In a capital-based economy, this is a powerful indicator that measures that improve accessibility and opportunity are consequently bound to generate benefits for the entire Ontario population.

Dignity: What Does It Mean?

The central premise of this book is that disabled individuals in Canada are currently not accorded the level of dignity to which they are entitled under the law. It is important to be clear, however, in what this legal provision consists and how it is meant to be applied.

The promotion and protection of individual dignity is anchored in the equality provisions of the Charter of Rights and Freedoms of the Constitution of Canada. Section 15 of the Charter states:

(1) Every individual is equal before and under the law and has the right to the equal protection and equal benefit of the law without discrimination and, in particular, without discrimination based on race, national or ethnic origin, colour, religion, sex, age or mental or physical disability.

(2) Subsection (1) does not preclude any law, program or activity that has as its object the amelioration of conditions of disadvantaged individuals or groups, including those that are disadvantaged because of race, national or ethnic origin, colour, religion, sex, age or mental or physical disability.

As noted by the Supreme Court of Canada, at the heart of discrimination is the question of human dignity. The Court stated:

In general terms, the purpose of s.15 (1) is to prevent the violation of essential human dignity and freedom through the imposition of disadvantage, stereotyping, or political or social prejudice, and to promote a society in which all persons enjoy equal recognition at law as human beings or as members of Canadian society, equally capable and equally deserving of concern, respect and consideration... Human dignity means that an individual or group feels self-respect and self-worth. It is concerned with physical and psychological integrity and empowerment. Human dignity is harmed by unfair treatment premised upon personal traits or circumstances that do not relate to individual needs, capacities, or merits... Human dignity is harmed when individuals and groups are marginalized, ignored, or devalued, and is enhanced when laws recognize the full place of all individuals and groups within Canadian society.[3]

Dignity, then, is understood as stemming from the equality provisions of the Charter of Rights and Freedoms. "Equality" itself is an exceptionally broad concept that is not easy to define and is indeed frequently interpreted in a variety of mutually exclusive ways. In this instance, however, it is explicitly identified in terms of autonomy and self-determination. The latter two notions can also be subject to differing interpretations but in the present context are intended to refer to qualities expressive of an authentic self. A self may be said to be "authentic" whenever it consistently demonstrates a capacity for self-reflection and shows an ability to act competently on whatever set of objectives and values it freely chooses as its own. To be autonomous and self-determined, therefore, means to be in rational control of the choices and actions of everyday life. Moreover, an autonomous self should rightfully expect the regard and respect of other autonomous agents for the ability to decide for one's self, to control life and deal with the consequences of one's own actions. As would be expected, this is a goal shared among individuals with a disability.

Conversely, where the self does not enjoy the gift of self-reflection and is unable to act cogently on its own freely chosen set of ends, authenticity is lost and the self cannot be considered an autonomous self-determined being. There are different reasons for a loss of autonomy. Some individuals lack a recognized level of rational self-control due to youth or intellectual impairment and in these cases external intervention in their lives is accepted as normative in law. When, however, other persons intrude to control or direct the everyday life of a person who is physically disabled then the intercession must be deemed morally illegitimate. Proper respect for the autonomy and dignity of people with disabilities must be preserved in the face of paternalistic interventions.

It is important to emphasize that the autonomy requirement contained in the Supreme Court's ruling only represents the minimum requirement for a

---

3. *Law v. Canada (Minister of Employment and Immigration)* (1999), 170 D.L.R. (4th) 1 paragraphs 4 and 53.

self to be accorded dignity. The Court is aware that the social and material circumstances of individuals substantially diverge and that many do not have access to the resources necessary to satisfy their goals and ambitions. This may translate into a state concern for personal or public safety. This is often exemplified where a person is experiencing an acute period of psychiatric illness. For this reason, it is recognized that some forms of external intervention into the lives of individuals is legitimate if this intervention serves to sustain and extend the autonomy and dignity of the self. As the Court noted:

> It is inappropriate to attempt to confine analysis under s.15 (1) of the Charter to a fixed and limited formula. A purposive and contextual approach to discrimination analysis is to be preferred, in order to permit the realization of the strong remedial purpose of the equality guarantee, and to avoid the pitfalls of a formalistic or mechanical approach.[4]

When society often evolves to a more egalitarian view that is acceptable of a diverse community, persons with a disability can look forward to benefiting from a "contextual approach" to an equality analysis. It is, however, the very fact that the judiciary has chosen to consider the actuality of the broader community in which disabled persons wish to assert their rights that there remains a sobering anchor that prevents radical change. Still, most disability rights activists turn to the courts and human rights tribunals for the application of what is frequently considered the most progressive measures articulated in the advancement of disability rights.

More will be discussed later, with particular reference to the Supreme Court of Canada's evolution of the "duty to accommodate" persons with a disability within the rubric of constitutional guarantees of equality. Ways that dignity and autonomy for people with disabilities can be promoted in order to embrace more wide-ranging and substantial aspects of their lives will also be explored.

Discrimination

In the past few years, the concept of "discrimination" has attained an important foothold in the consciousness of Canadian citizens. This process of development has been irregular and episodic, but the reasons behind it are not difficult to discern. Newspapers and television news broadcasts make frequent

---

4. *Law v. Canada (Minister of Employment and Immigration) (1999), 170 D.L.R. (4th) 1.*

reference to incidents and events in which individuals have reported they have been the subject of one or other form of discrimination. For example, we will frequently read or hear that a shooting was racially motivated. We may also hear that, after some protest, the problem has been fixed.

As individuals, only a few sad Canadians on the periphery of society find contentment in referring to themselves as "racists" or "bigots." As for many of the rest, they would be deeply offended if they were ever actually accused of practicing discrimination and are genuinely surprised when their jokes and sniggers about the new female office administrator are not always taken in the intended spirit of "good fun."

Equally significant, is the fact that "discrimination" is widely judged as a fairly easy word to understand. People have an intrinsic sense of its meaning. In much the same vein as terms like "robbery" or "murder," most members of the public believe they have a reasonably good idea of what it means although they might be a little more hard-pressed to provide a legal definition of the term or to explain how discrimination relates to broader ethical issues such as those encompassing personal dignity.

Furthermore, should one consider the dearth of literature respecting disability issues in any national party's platform in the federal elections of the past ten years, and the fact that the Liberal Party's Renewal Commission has ignored disability issues, then one may conclude that a majority of Canadians believe that discrimination and the denial of dignity respecting persons with a disability is not a burning social issue.

To the credit of the NDP, Conservative and Liberal parties, they do support the development of a Canadians with Disabilities Act. As will be discussed later, the *Accessibility for Ontarians with Disabilities Act* has had its growing pains, but I remain optimistic that comprehensive human rights legislation protecting persons with a disability may have great potential for building a more inclusive society. My hope is that the current federal government can move forward on the proposed legislation before they are in another election campaign due to the tenuous nature of being a minority government in the House of Commons.

Although, broadly speaking, many may think that the problem of discrimination in Canada is resolved, such conclusions are rejected by those distinct communities that are affected by prejudice. Clearly, Canada is not the Deep

South of the United States during the years of racial segregation, much less South Africa in the era of apartheid where state policy clearly segregated and subordinated a group based on a personal characteristic. However, to a member of a marginalized group, isolation and exclusion is virtually palpable. Too often the accepted norm of the "drunken Indian" or welfare recipient who "went on disability," and other profoundly negative stereotypes, allows a perpetuation of myths that creates an invisible or virtual segregation.

What Discrimination Is and Is Not

The widespread and, one might suggest, wilful blindness to the reality of discrimination and its concomitant attack on human dignity is a central and recurring theme throughout this book. For the moment, however, I want to begin with another noticeable aspect of the term discrimination as it now popularly occurs in Canadian society. What I am referring to is the sheer repetitive use of the idiom in day-to-day conversation and its repeated application to social and cultural contexts in which it manifestly does not pertain.

If a majority of Canadians seem willing to deny that they actively practice discrimination against identifiable minorities, then more and more of them also seem to want to claim that they are its victims. Increasingly, it seems, the word is invoked whenever anyone feels grieved, slighted, or misunderstood, and as a result there has now arisen a real danger that the concept of discrimination has become seriously devalued. The practical import of this state of affairs is that the case of a woman who suffers genuine discrimination and loss of dignity through the sexually suggestive comments of her supervisor may not be properly differentiated from that of the woman who is merely upset at her poor performance review. As the boy who cried wolf found out to his cost, use any term frivolously or, in the case of discrimination, without enough care and precision and the consequences can be tragic. With this, I will also assert that the assumption and application of rights is a two-way street where neither the bigot nor the whiner is of any utility in the debate. Essentially with rights come responsibilities.

So what exactly is discrimination and how as Canadians should we understand its proper meaning and application? References to discrimination are found in the Charter of Rights and Freedoms, Canadian Human Rights Act, and provincial Human Rights Codes. In general terms, discrimination is defined as any practice or behaviour that, either intentionally or not, imposes a disadvantage or some other negative effect on certain specified individuals or groups. It does so on the grounds that such persons possess certain identifiable characteristics or traits that are unique to their individuality or group membership. In Ontario, these traits (or what are termed in the province's Human Rights Code, "protected grounds") encompass race, ancestry, place of origin, colour, ethnic origin, citizenship, creed, sex, sexual orientation, age, record of offences, marital status, same-sex partnership status, family status, disability, or any other analogous ground. The principal effect of discrimination on its subject parties is to deny or restrict full or meaningful access to one or more social good, service, benefit, opportunity, or amenity that is otherwise freely accessible to all other members of the community.

Furthermore, the practice of discrimination forms the grounds for a range of differential perceptions that are ultimately grounded in the belief that the bearers of one or other of these identified traits are in some significant sense less capable or less worthy of recognition and respect as persons than other individuals in society. So, for example, the discriminatory belief that women or persons from a particular ethnic background are physically weaker than white Caucasian males, often gives rise to the further idea that the former do not deserve to be paid the same as the latter. Similarly, Canadian society is currently infused with a belief structure that considers people with physical disabilities as individuals incapable of applying themselves to either the practical tasks of everyday life or, more generally, of adhering to the standards and principles that define social worth and cultural significance in Canadian society. This discriminatory attitude (or "able-ism" as it is sometimes called) is defined by its focus on the differences that exist in the bodily constitution of persons with disabilities. Rather than recognize that the body of *every* Canadian is "different" from that of everyone else, the body of a person with a physical disability is viewed as a sign that the individual is not a fully functioning, autonomous self; not completely a character capable of exercising freedom of choice in the pursuit of personal responsibility and self-determination.

Before looking at the parameters of the concept of discrimination in more detail, there are a couple of points that should be emphasized. In the first place, it should be obvious that the particular characteristic or trait that is identified as the basis for excluding its bearer from certain social goods and benefits is, in itself, without any foundation. There is no basis in reality that leads to the conclusion that a person who lacks the physical ability to be independently mobile enjoys any less intrinsic moral worth than other human beings.

Having said that, it is also important to understand that the characteristics and traits identified as socially undesirable cannot be considered merely the haphazard and uninformed imaginings of lonely individuals. On the contrary, it seems evident, from even the most cursory inspection of the history of discrimination in Western societies, that there exist a number of persistent themes that recur frequently, identifying the same individuals or groups as objects of exclusion from society's goods and benefits; principally, women, those of particular racial or ethnic backgrounds, gays and lesbians. There also exists an evolving history of discrimination and exclusion against people with disabilities. The roots of discrimination lie in a series of complex structures encompassing socio-economic factors, power relationships, and dominant ideologies. It is these structures, which have historically prevailed in Western societies that have resulted in, amongst other things, the methodical segregation of minority groups from effective and meaningful control of their own lives. The very fact that discrimination and exclusion continue to exist today is a clear demonstration of the unrelenting dominance of these structures and their continued influence over every aspect of everyday life. If people with disabilities are ever to be free of discrimination and regain the dignity proper to them as persons, then it is the influence of these structures as generators of discrimination and exclusion that must be addressed.

Another point about discrimination that should be mentioned is that it can be practised in a number of different ways. For their part, Canadian courts have traditionally recognized two main forms of discriminatory practice that are critical to understanding their conceptual approach. The first, and perhaps most straightforward, variant is known as "direct" discrimination, which, as the name suggests, applies to any act of discrimination that is manifestly blatant or overt. For instance, if an employer in Toronto refused to hire someone for the simple reason that he or she belonged to one of the protected groups specified in the Ontario Human Rights Code then his discrimination would be direct.

In contrast to this, a second type, known as "adverse impact" discrimination (also sometimes known as "indirect" or "systemic" discrimination) occurs whenever an entity such as a company or service provider implements a rule or regulation that is intended in good faith to apply to all employees, but that nonetheless imposes a discriminatory burden on one or more groups specified in the Human Rights Code. The group or groups in question have a particular characteristic that imposes some special requirement, obligation, or penalty on its bearers that is not visited on other members of the community. An example of adverse impact discrimination would be the requirement in a job contract to work on a certain day of the week when members of a religious group were unable to do so for spiritual reasons. Similarly, a person using a wheelchair would be discriminated against after this fashion if the actual location of the job he or she was applying for (and was otherwise qualified for) was physically inaccessible due to some feature in the layout of the place of work. Both forms of discrimination are illegal, according to a Supreme Court of Canada decision made in 1999.[5]

Prejudice

Another aspect of the concept of discrimination worth noting, and which may suggest further limitations to the Supreme Court's apparent progressive thinking, is the several similar and associated terms for discrimination that are frequently substituted in the course of day-to-day conversation but which actually enjoy their own quite specific legal meanings. One term that is commonly used as a surrogate for discrimination is "prejudice." Closer examination shows, however, that whereas the former is defined as a kind of practice or behaviour that imposes disadvantages on others because of certain proscribed characteristics or traits, prejudice is better understood as a type of unfavourable opinion that is based either on insufficient information or immaterial considerations about the object of the belief in question.

In other words, while discrimination is an activity carried out in the social arena, prejudice is a more personal affair that concerns judgments about others that need never be publicly uttered. Moreover, whereas the practice of discrimination arises from a historically structured nexus of socio-economic forces, power relations, and dominant ideologies, prejudice is frequently rooted in the individual's lack of education and poor or inadequate socialization into the community.

---

5. *British Columbia (Public Service Employee Relations Commission) v. British Columbia Government and Service Employees' Union [1999] 3 S.C.R. 3.*

As such, it has sometimes been considered a more subtle and insidious affair than the practice of discrimination itself. If this sounds surprising, it is worth remembering that at least discrimination can be officially legislated against and penalties for its practice more or less enthusiastically enforced. Prejudice, on the other hand, often lurks deep in the mind of the individual, only to emerge without warning in the most unexpected contexts. It's a largely unseen and unarticulated peril that must be addressed in fresh and innovative ways. "Racism," another term often serving as a proxy for discrimination, can be thought of properly as a species of both discrimination and prejudice. Based on an ideological belief system which views certain racial or ethnic groups as inherently superior to others, racism may take form either as an exclusionary practice or as a set of personal beliefs and assumptions. In either case it is one of the more blatant attacks on human dignity in contemporary Canadian society.

Harassment

Prejudice is frequently layered by the closely related term to discrimination, "harassment." This species of exclusionary practice refers to a situation in which someone either utters aggravating comments or engages in annoying behaviours related to one of the protected grounds of the Human Rights Code and that realistically is or should be known to be offensive or unwelcome to the person addressed. Distasteful "jokes," inappropriate remarks, out-of-place observations, unpleasant banter, objectionable chit-chat, bothersome conduct, aggravating manner, infuriating demeanour, and obnoxious disposition are only several of the many ways harassment becomes a daily reality in the workplace and the community at large. Collectively it creates what is known as a "poisoned environment" in which persons or groups protected by the Human Rights Code are made subject to real or perceived inequalities in any setting where others are not the focus of similar treatment. Innocent quips around the water cooler such as "a woman's place is rightfully in the home" often goes a long way towards turning the workplace setting into an environment where the dignity of all women is consistently compromised.

Like the great majority of other legal concepts, terms like discrimination, prejudice and harassment are of course always open to conjecture and interpretation. Part of the problem lies in the nature of language itself. Rich and expressive as the English and French languages are, legislators have only a limited number of verbs and adjectives to describe the multi-faceted dimensions of discrimination and exclusion. Similarly, lawyers and Human Rights Tribunals are faced with a restricted sum of possible interpretations that can reasonably be placed on the rules and regulations governing this issue.

No fair-minded person would deny that there are a considerable number of cases of discrimination or harassment. However, these are not the instances that cause public concern or, more importantly, the impetus for debate so that we may further refine our collective understanding of this most fundamental of social concerns. Accordingly it is to the "grey areas" that attention must be turned; to those areas that we overlook not because we covertly desire to maintain exclusionary barriers against protected persons and groups but, more dismally, because we genuinely cannot see that the society we believe to be fair and just continues to exert intolerable burdens on many of our most vulnerable citizens.

Focusing solely on the issue of discrimination will not be sufficient in itself to address the issue of dignity for protected persons and groups. That this is so may be seen when we consider the following: Let us imagine that when we wake up tomorrow the federal government and provincial legislatures have decided to create new legislation that comprehensively addresses all aspects of discrimination in Canada. Assisted by some particularly erudite lawyers, this legislation cuts to the core of all the marginal and difficult cases and proposes principles that inclusively attend to everyone's concerns. Imagine also that a new will and determination takes hold amongst those responsible for applying and implementing this legislation so that each case is resolved in accordance with the Wisdom of Solomon. Were all this to happen, and the issue of discrimination truly engaged with, then what would be the situation of protected persons and groups in general and people with disabilities in particular?

There is no doubt that an effective legislative agenda and program of enforcement would do a great deal to improve the overall social situation of people with disabilities. Indeed, many would argue that we were realizing the fruits of progressive legislation. The removal of discriminatory practices and behaviours, and associated forms of harassment would at the very least remove the overt exclusionary barriers that currently still exist. It would restore to persons with disabilities full access to the range of social goods, benefits, opportunities, and amenities currently enjoyed by other members of the community.

Whether this access is sufficient to restore parity and equality between persons with disabilities and other members of society is another question altogether. Put another way, even if what is currently defined as discrimination and harassment were completely eradicated tomorrow, that does not mean that individuals with disabilities would automatically regain the dignity that is due to them as persons. Dignity cannot simply be attained through a more inclusive legal definition of discrimination and harassment, regardless of how comprehensive that definition is and how effective its means of enforcement. In short, more effective legislation will not guarantee that persons with disabilities will receive the recognition and respect that is their due as members of society.

Learned Subordination

The attentive reader will have noticed that in the last couple of paragraphs I have been pointing out the intrinsic inadequacy of more effective legal definitions of discrimination and harassment. I deliberately omitted reference to the term "prejudice," which, it will be recalled, referred specifically to cases where someone held unfavourable opinions about protected persons and groups on the grounds of insufficient information or immaterial considerations.

The notion of prejudice is important in the present regard because, in the absence of some kind of Orwellian dystopia, it is difficult to see how any governing body could formulate judicially sound legislation regulating the opinions that some people hold. Certainly, as was implied earlier, a more liberal education and more enlightened socialization would undoubtedly contest much of what currently passes as prejudice. But changing peoples' opinions is a more protracted and complex process than altering, say, hiring practices. In the meantime, the undercurrent of thoughtlessness and insensitivity that feeds the river of prejudice continues unchecked. This might be dismissed as no more than another one of those intractable social issues if it wasn't for the deep and immediate consequences prejudice has on persons with disabilities.

As noted earlier, prejudicial opinions are frequently held in private and needn't find wide public expression. That doesn't mean to say that persons with disabilities aren't acutely aware of the plethora of disinformation and erroneous perception that informs a significant part of the general public's awareness of their physical, intellectual, and material conditions of existence. The public's ignorance (and there really is no other word for it) not only engenders various forms of marginalization but, in a cruel reversal, serves to internalize the message of exclusion to the disabled themselves. Persons with disabilities are not just faced with the evident forms of discrimination and harassment that emerge in the material reality of everyday life. There is also a psychological reality, which, prompted by an awareness of the pervasiveness of prejudicial opinion, causes persons with disabilities to effectively minimize their own expectations for equality and dignity. Persons with disabilities frequently lack confidence in themselves as persons. Rather than celebrate who they are as autonomous beings worthy of the recognition and respect of other members of the community, they choose to construct themselves entirely in terms of what they take to be society's negative estimation of disability. If a woman with a disability suspects that it is the opinion of many in the community that her disability renders her intrinsically unable to function as a self-determining entity (and hence undeserving of social esteem) then it is not difficult to understand why, over time, she can come to believe that opinion is true. Taken to its logical extension, one can see how such prejudice can serve to limit the psychosexual expression of the self (for men or women), and deny the right to marriage or family.

The kind of self-doubt and insecurity that I am trying to describe here is rife throughout the disabled community and constitutes for individuals perhaps the single greatest obstacle to the establishment of dignity. But how is this self-doubt and feeling of insecurity to be understood? This is an important question because unless we understand why people with disabilities feel about themselves in the way they do then it becomes very difficult to suggest any practical or realistic alternatives for bringing about constructive change. So, how do the attitudes and opinions constituting society's negative estimation of disability arise? What mechanisms are at work in Canadian society that cause persons with disabilities to doubt their own self-worth?

Stigmatization

In 1963, Canadian-born sociologist Erving Goffman published *Stigma: Notes on the Management of Spoiled Identity*. Goffman's aim was to explain how a particular trait or character attribute, which he termed "stigma," functioned in society to indicate those undesired differences that serve to separate and differentiate certain identified individuals from others in the mainstream. He defined stigma as an "attribute that is deeply discrediting" and one that reduced its bearer "from a whole and usual person to a tainted, discounted one."[6] Thus, according to Goffman, a stigma is something like a sign or mark of a feature that society treats as actually existing in the person rather than simply a label or description that is attached *post factum* to the individual. This sign or mark may relate to a specific feature of a person; for example, race or religion or to particular aspects of character (as when we say someone is either inherently dishonest or is weak-willed) and also, Goffman stated, to the physical and intellectual disabilities of individuals. In this manner, the term "stigma" serves to draw attention to facets of the situation of protected persons and groups that is quite different from that suggested by "discrimination" and "harassment." The latter are terms that are used to describe the behaviours of the originators of the practices of exclusion and rejection. "Stigma," on the other hand, expresses the condition of persons and groups who are the subjects of such behaviours.

How does a person or group come to be stigmatized? There are a number of aspects to the process that are all grounded in, what can be termed, the social selection of difference. Difference defines individuals and surrounds them in every aspect of their lives. Significantly, however, some differences are socially more important than others. The fact that the car I drive is blue rather than red is of no real public consequence; however, the fact that it is a Ford and not a Porsche can have significant social resonance. Generally speaking, in Western cultures, it is those differences that in some measure come to enhance the individual's personal well-being and social status (for instance, youth, wealth, good health, graduate education, reputable employment) that are accorded a positive standing. Those differences that have the opposite effect on well-being and status (old age, poverty, serious illness, disability, minimal education, low-paying job) are consistently regarded as indicators of some fault or failing on the part of the individual concerned. The assumption that these (and similar) differences are the differences that really matter in society has become so ingrained in public consciousness that, for most people, it has become inconceivable that the supposition might not be true. And if this sounds like an overly sweeping generalization about the nature of social reality then it stands to be emphasized that this simplification is quite deliberate. A reduction of the

---

6.   Erving Goffman, *Stigma: Notes on the Management of Spoiled Identity* (Touchstone, reissue edition 1986).

intricacies and complexities of the social body to the austerity of black and white categories is an integral part of the process of stigmatization.

Goffman then went on to suggest a second aspect of the stigmatization process in which persons negatively labelled by the community as socially "different" (such as the old, poor, or disabled) are linked through the established structure of cultural beliefs to some further set of undesirable characteristics or attributes. That is to say, individuals who exist, as it were, "out of the ordinary" are not only identified for their deviance from societal norms but also become stereotyped in some fashion as ethically inadequate. It is this latter deviant characteristic that then becomes the principal centre of consideration and through which the community's reactions are phrased. For example, penury and deprivation are not only viewed as personal failings on the part of those denied effective access to the social means of wealth creation, it commonly also leads to a stereotyped view of the poor as apathetic, shiftless, and lazy. Similarly, persons with intellectual disabilities are not just assessed as lacking the wherewithal to act as independent agents in society but are frequently also stereotyped as "unstable" and a "danger" to other members of the community.

The linking of negative labels with detrimental attributes leads, in turn, to a third aspect of stigmatization: a contrived division of the community into "us" (that is, those individuals who hold to culturally determined norms of personal well-being and social status) and "them" (those who fail to adhere to such norms and who have been stereotyped as undesirable). The existence of this schism is important because it is this perception of difference that founds the belief that those persons or groups negatively labelled ("them") are, in a very real and concrete sense, fundamentally unlike everyone else ("us"). They are, quite simply, different types of people belonging to a separate order of humanity. Indeed, in its most extreme historical manifestations, some individuals and groups have been perceived to be so unlike "us" as not to be thought of as human at all (for instance, Africans during the time of slavery, Jews in Nazi Germany and, more recently, Bosnians during the wars of the Yugoslav secession).

More commonly, however, targeted groups and individuals are treated on an everyday basis as though they physically embodied the attribute with which they have been labelled. Thus persons with disabilities are frequently referred to in casual conversation as being disabled. The significance of this choice of language becomes apparent when compared to the idiom employed in discussing other types of medical pathology. For example, a person with cancer is not normally described as being cancerous but rather as a person who has cancer. In other words, our shared cultural norms dictate that persons who have cancer will be permitted to remain as one of "us" (albeit as an individual with a serious affliction). On the other hand, persons with disabilities (those who "are" disabled or handicapped) will forever remain one of "them" evermore outside the norms and values of mainstream society.

It is worth emphasizing at this juncture that the three faces of stigmatization just sketched depend for their operational authority in Canadian society on the defining hierarchy of social relations and distribution of economic power. What this means at the end of the day is that the ability to stigmatize depends fundamentally on the access that select fractions of the community enjoy to continuously shape and affect social norms and values. It is this access that allows them to present their culturally determined ideas of personal and social well-being as valid for society as a whole and, at the same time, permits them to condemn any deviance from these norms as the traits of "others" not fully affiliated in the community. For this reason, it is not hard to see why the process of stigmatization is so very much a one-way street. Unlike the rich, the young, and the able-bodied, the poor, the old, and persons with disabilities, have no access to the societal resources necessary to validate their understandings of personal well-being and social worth as important for the community as a whole. And if anyone should still imagine that the process of stigmatizing others is no more than a kind of run-of-the-mill snobbery or conceit then it is worth bearing in mind that the type of social power that it takes to stigmatize others is precisely the type of power that confers control over the critical life-affirming areas of human existence (for instance, health, education, employment, and housing). Stigma is not simply a matter of calling other people names; more fundamentally, it's about regulating admission to many of the most important sources of human welfare.

But the most important aspect of stigma is the effect that it has on its targeted individuals and groups (such as those with disabilities). Persons who are stigmatized are faced with invasive and never-ending reminders of their inferior position within Canadian society. In turn, this not only facilitates the forms of discrimination and harassment discussed earlier but also leads persons with disabilities to internalize feelings of shame, humiliation, embarrassment, awkwardness, unworthiness, and discomfort. Awareness of the stigmatizing labels and associated negative attributes attached to them inevitably comes to have a serious effect on the self-perception of persons with disabilities. Many eventually come to believe the veracity of these assertions and in their own position as "outsiders" living precariously on the margins of mainstream society. It is this lack of self-confidence in their own persons as integrated, autonomous, and dignified selves that colours all aspects of their social relations with others and frustrates the possibility of broad and meaningful change.

Conclusion

The widespread belief in Canadian society that the provisions contained in both the Charter of Rights and Freedoms and provincial Human Rights Codes have largely won the fight against discrimination is an illusion. This has arisen from a perception that the law, or rightly stated "human rights law" is a panacea. The problem of turning the tide of discrimination is much more complicated than that. If used in a singular or exclusive fashion, the law can serve to be mutually exclusive to other efforts to promote the rights and dignity of persons with a disability. As will be articulated throughout this book, dignity and equality arise from exercising the Six Degrees (or elements) of Dignity in concert. When these varying aspects of the effort toward equality and dignity move forward in an integrated fashion, meaningful progress can be achieved. The struggle for dignity for all has only just begun.

↜

CHAPTER 3

Dignity in Public Perception

Dante Hicks: The guy's in a wheelchair.
Randal Graves: I know. That's why I call him "crippie-boy."
from *Clerks II*, screenplay by Kevin Smith

SUCH CONCEPTS AS DISCRIMINATION, prejudice, harassment, internalized subordination, and stigma play a powerful role in entrenching marginalization of a group, and this is frequently experienced by the disability community. Changing public perceptions is a critical step in removing these historically held norms.

Perception of the disabled self is a complicated process with its own dynamic and history. A common thread of this history is a systematic denial of free choice and the imposition upon the disabled of physical and psychological constraints incompatible with their dignity as persons. This chapter will consider several areas where disability issues and public perception meet and often clash: stereotypical images of disability in mass media and popular art forms; fundraising for disability causes; and the administration of criminal justice on persons with a disability.

The Socio-Historic Context of Disability in Canada

Able-bodied individuals have historically controlled where disabled persons live and how they receive their basic needs. The historically linked causal factors to this loss of autonomy outline the critical need for an "independent living lens" in reversing entrenched discriminatory historical norms.

In the Middle Ages, disabled persons were usually cared for by family members with support from the church and community. These developments were the precursors to what commentators have described as the charity model, which continues to have a powerful impact even today. In effect, the disabled person is considered an object to be pitied because he or she could neither fit into a society mainstream nor care for his or herself. Providing a donation to support that individual may bring the donor positive community response, cleanse a sense of shame, or assist in having a good afterlife. A contemporary example of this form of objectification can typically be found in a variety of telethons.

Also in the Middle Ages, disabled persons were persecuted because superstition suggested that their disability was God's will, or a result of demonic possession. Thus they were to be feared and, with this, pressed to the margins of society. While many may wish to believe that Canadians have evolved in their thinking beyond such an irrational fear-based view of disability and disablement, the reaction of several sectors to the AIDS epidemic in the 1980s may suggest otherwise. Due to ignorance and/or a narrow world view, persons with HIV/AIDS were reviled for their disease and/or lifestyle choices that may have contributed to acquiring the virus.

The Age of Enlightenment in the late 18th century changed the way that persons with a disability were cared for and housed. Based on a model that was thought to be rational, there was little room for anyone who deviated from the norm or was not considered to have sufficient labour market potential. Society's response was to build large institutions where persons with a disability were accommodated. Other groups pushed to the social margins within this paradigm were orphans, single mothers, the poor (in Victorian "work houses" or debtors' prisons), and later, able-bodied Aboriginal children in the residential school system. With the exception of the very wealthy, who could afford private care, this systemic approach continued into the 20th century.

A further outcome of the institutionalization of disabled persons was the full control of all daily activities, and consequent loss of independence. Disability rights commentators refer to this as the medical model. The decision makers within this model were usually physicians who promised to cure or change the symptomatic manifestations of disability. As a result, disabled persons were defined by their biomedical condition to the exclusion of their psychosocial selves. Treatment of that condition was considered a benevolent rationale for the containment of the disability community, but it resulted in profound disempowerment that remains a matter of concern into the 21st century.

World War II was to mark a shift toward a more autonomous lifestyle for persons with a disability. Firstly, basic human rights and civil liberties were enshrined in the United Nations Universal Declaration on Human Rights. Secondly, medical advances were providing greater quality care and allowing persons with disabling medical conditions to live much longer than before. Finally, many war veterans returned home with devastating disabilities. They were unwilling to live in paternalistic institutional care and, because of the sacrifices they had made for their country, there was a strong public sentiment that their wishes should be honoured. It may be argued that this was the genesis of a perception within the disability community and broader society that persons with a disability deserved equality and dignity.

During the last quarter of the 20th century, several disability organizations adopted agendas that were consistent with the civil rights movements of the 1950s through 1970s. The common position of these organizations was that the dignity of persons with a disability must be recognized and that that full participation in the socio-economic and cultural benefits of its citizenry was a basic human right rather than abstract concept. With respect to persons with a disability, this broad effort to be full participants in society was given the term "independent living movement."

These deeply entrenched historical norms have had a profound impact in denying autonomy, choice, and equality to persons with a disability. They have experienced institutionalization, poverty, and subordination with its residual effects still seen today in a society that all too often marginalizes persons with a disability. As the chart below shows, there are a number of distinct perspectives in this continuum. However, the central tenet of the independent living movement is to promote solutions to that inequality.

Five Views of Rights and Responsibilities

	Rights and Responsibilities	Results
CHARITY Past	People have the RIGHT to hope for help Those who have been fortunate have the RESPONSIBILITY to give money	Encourages isolation, prejudice, hopelessness, helplessness People having no voice **Nevertheless, individuals and groups supported that would not have flourished otherwise**
MEDICAL Present	People have the RIGHT to medical help The medical profession has the RESPONSIBILITY to decide if you are sick	Passivity Isolation No attention to social needs **Nevertheless evolves other strategies: chronic and palliative care that values individuals**
REHABILITATION Present	People have the RIGHT to work Vocational rehabilitation professionals have the RESPONSIBILITY to decide how work can be done and who can do it	Tied to economical policy Inefficient Disenfranchising Dependency Hostility and frustration Jumping through the hoops **Nevertheless connected the individual with social reality**
SOCIO/POLITICAL Present	People have the RIGHT to participate in society Government has the RESPONSIBILITY to make sure laws and programs facilitate the participation	Criticizes medical and economical model to excess Lacks cohesion Conflict Rights can be wiped away Short-term focus to solve long-term problems **Nevertheless prepares the way for more co-operative models**
INDEPENDENT LIVING Future	RIGHTS and RESPONSIBILITIES are shared, learned, supported, and changed in CO-OPERATION with the community, with leadership from everyone devoted to the common good from the federal government and all others interested in building a country based on inclusion, equity, affordability, and justice	**CITIZENSHIP**

While facing entrenched historical links to discrimination, individuals with disabilities are advancing human rights norms to protect their dignity in the 21st century. Perhaps the song is correct—freedom is about having nothing left to lose—but the history of the disability civil rights movement has been about attempts to gain selfhood and social inclusion after persistent extreme objectification. It is in that socio-historic context that persons with disabilities often feel that they must determine how to assert their human rights and promote an equal society.

Popular Culture and Media Portrayals of Disability

Notwithstanding advances in changing historical linkages to discrimination, PWDs continue to face many challenges to attaining dignity due to the depiction of disability in the media and other forms of popular culture. Newspaper stories about people with disabilities fall into a number of types. There are stories about:

- Courageous people with disabilities who have battled to overcome obstacles or who *somehow* "manage to hold down a job";
- Medical breakthroughs that could benefit people with disabilities;
- People with disabilities fundraising for good causes;
- People whose operations have gone wrong—with an emphasis on lawsuits and monetary awards, rather than the individual's injury and pain.

There is very little coverage of the way society treats people with disabilities, and there are very few stories written by or for people with disabilities.

Literature and art typically portray physical deformity, chronic illness, or any visible defect as symbolic of an evil, malevolent nature and the character's monstrous behaviour. Lawbreakers are frequently ugly and deformed; heroes and heroines are beautiful and graceful. From Snow White's seven dwarves and the Munchkins over the rainbow, to Frankenstein and Darth Vader, the cinema both sentimentalizes and demonizes physical difference.

Also, film and television employ the metaphor of disabled persons as helpless victims. For example, roughing up a "cripple" illustrates that the villain is exceptionally evil. Television tends to endow disabled protagonists with superhuman characteristics, for example, the "Bionic Man" or "Ironside," the brilliant—paraplegic—San Francisco detective.

Physical ugliness and physical differences are often associated with media depictions of violence, crime, and horror. Consider the villains portrayed in the popular movies *Batman* and *Spiderman*. Cartoons and comic strips carry hurtful and discriminatory language and images. Words such as "stupid moron," "idiot," "crazy," are common jargon. Everyday words referring to specific conditions have become curse words, and stereotypes of disability are reinforced. However, the above is nothing new; one may be reminded of how Shakespeare portrayed Richard III as a hunchback to indicate both his physical and psychological deformity.

Recently, there have been some attempts, in plays and films, to present more sympathetic views of people with disabilities. Disabled persons are being depicted as "incidental" characters—neither hero nor victim. The elderly, the ugly, the obese, are seen more often as "normal." "Sue Thomas, F.B. Eye" is a criminal profiler who is deaf. The movies "Children of a Lesser God," "A Beautiful Mind," and "I Am Sam" portrayed sensitive and realistic stories of the deaf, schizophrenia, and developmental disabilities.

The media is beginning to move away from depicting the disabled in simplistic black and white terms, but it is still a long way from normalizing its portrayal of disability. People with disabilities could be shown living and working in a variety of situations, with diverse responsibilities, and not necessarily overcoming great odds in their pursuit of an independent life. Judicious use of terminology and visual images of people with disabilities can help fashion a more realistic picture of people with disabilities as "ordinary" people.

Theatre By and For Persons With Disabilities

Despite the havoc the media can wreak in public portrayals of disability, PWDs can assume control of their own cultural lives. Since 1977, the innovative National Theatre Workshop of the Handicapped[7] has given some one thousand young Americans with varying disabilities a voice and training that enables them to provide for themselves. Courses in areas such as music, voice,

---

7. You may find out more information about the National Theatre Workshop of the Handicapped by going to their website at http://www.ntwh.org.

dance, playwriting, and theatre management under the guidance of professional staff give students self-esteem, confidence, fulfillment, and dignity.

Its founder, Rick Curry, conceived of the now three-year residential program, after he was bumped from auditioning for a hamburger commercial because he had only one arm. At the time, Curry was a Jesuit brother and impoverished doctoral candidate at New York University. He is certain that he was turned away from auditioning due to prejudice, not merit or talent.

The underlying philosophy of the workshop is that artists, especially artists with disabilities, see the world from a unique perspective. Students come together to learn, but also to teach one another and their audiences how to accept disability and also celebrate it.

While professional integration to film and theatre remains extremely difficult for persons with a disability across Canada and the United States, there are efforts that are taking a toehold on the industry for actors, models, and writers with a disability. For example, Sue Charness, of Charness Talent in Toronto, is a talent agent that exclusively represents persons with a disability. While we may not be finding persons with a disability in leading roles in Hollywood films, Ms. Charness, through charm and tenacity, has been able to place her clients in commercials, films, magazines, and major Toronto stage productions for over ten years.

There is also the Los Angeles-based actor, producer, and director, Otto Felix, who owns and operates an acting studio on Santa Monica Boulevard in North Hollywood that is fully supportive of both able-bodied and disabled actors working together to develop their craft. I have attended several of Otto's workshops and have had the pleasure of observing the transformative nature of his skills as a teacher where he draws the acting talents of his students forward, and allows them to tap into their essential selves when creating a character for self-expression. As he often notes, acting is the one profession that is done best when nobody can notice that it is happening. He brings out the best in his actors so that they stop faking it and literally become the person whom they are presenting.

When teaching, Otto will sometimes quote Spencer Tracy who reportedly said that in order to act all you need to do is show up on time, know your lines, and hit your mark. He also refers to Steve McQueen who is quoted as saying that acting is like swallowing glass. That is the creative source that Otto really tries to tap into, where people break down the walls that they have been socialized to present, and engage in very real emotional and spiritual development through art. This is a universal human need—the need to create through expression of their soul. These actors do not differentiate between their physicality, but rather engage in the elevated purpose that is the truth of the beauty that is fine art.

It is through the efforts of workshops and people such as Sue Charness and Otto Felix that persons with a disability will be able to find the dignity of self-expression and have it take root in the cultural fabric of society. When disabled artists tell their story, false perceptions and negative stereotypes, such as pity, fear, bitterness, or the tragedy of disability, can melt away to present disability as simply what it is, part of the human condition.

Dignity, Donation, and the Allure of Cure

The news media promotes certain images of the disabled by covering selected events and ignoring others. Always on the scent of an image the public will find appealing, dog guides for people with severe sensory impairments have become photogenic symbols for disability.

While many marathoners crossed Canada to promote attention for select causes, by and large the media selected young, attractive men with dramatic visual disabilities to receive coordinated backing. Promoters and handlers "packaged" these youth and directed the publicity en route. This coverage pressured businesses and politicians to be seen giving generously to the hero's cause.

I experienced this when wheeling across Canada. The media became more attentive to my tour, as the story evolved to one of Dave Shannon, victim of spinal cord injury (SCI) pursuing the goal of a medical cure. But my vision was of a Canada that could collectively achieve its potential by reaping the reward of economic, social, and cultural contributions provided by persons with disabilities, and all groups. You could almost see the microphones drop when I attempted to articulate that dream, as opposed to a somewhat more absurd suggestion that, because I have SCI, I'm a second-class citizen and should dream to be whole again—in other words "normal" just like them.

The public continues to be subjected to fundraising telethons, which equate disability with childlike behaviour and an infantile bodily state, and display helpless children in a manner designed to evoke public pity and open viewers' wallets. Add to this "recipe" a celebrity host, music, and glitter, and supporting the disabled becomes television entertainment.

For many years Canada was considered an international leader in the promotion of rights and opportunities for the disabled. More recently, however, the impetus for imaginative and innovative change has faltered while the needs of other excluded and disadvantaged groups have come to the forefront of public awareness. Over the years, special interest groups that support various disabilities, such as the Council of Canadians with Disabilities, Canadian Association of Independent Living Centres, Canadian Association of Community Living, and others, have attempted to bridge the gap in an attempt to keep the dilemma facing the disability community on the political agenda. While the work these groups and associations have done is noteworthy, their efforts are often rendered redundant when they are forced to jockey against each other for government funding and support. As a result, the cause has become fractured among a plethora of groups whose goals and objectives often serve to work in opposition to each other. In the dog-eat-dog world of competitive fundraising, organizations with the most resourceful and effective public relations machines generally enjoy the lion's share of governmental funding and public support.

The Rick Hansen Institute provides a case in point. Hansen's 1985 "Man in Motion World Tour" was widely applauded and motivated public imagination to the tune of over $148 million dollars in donations to spinal cord injury research. While no one questions the sincerity of his accomplishments, Hansen's elevation to the status of civic icon has not been universally welcomed. In particular, other campaigners and activists for the disabled censure his prominence for attracting sponsorship and government support to the detriment of their own concerns. For example, in 2004 extended consultations between the federal government and disability advocates concerning the allocation of state funding came to an abrupt end. It was subsequently revealed that private discussions took place between then Prime Minister Jean Chrétien and Hansen, which resulted in a unilateral announcement to award the majority of available funds (some 15 million dollars) to the Rick Hansen Institute. Many in the disabled community were angry and disappointed at what they perceived was the cynical exploitation of Hansen's popularity both for the financial benefit of his own institute and for the enhancement of the government's public profile.

Of greater concern for disability advocates, however, is what they identify as the seriously misguided goals pursued by Hansen and a significant number of other leading charitable organizations. Briefly stated, the Rick Hansen Institute is dedicated to a single pursuit—that of improving the quality of life for those experiencing spinal cord injuries by "finding a cure." In other words, all of the considerable funds donated to Hansen are dedicated to the pursuit of a medical solution to the problem of disability. From this perspective, remedial medical intervention to restore the disabled individual to a "normal" condition is considered not only proper but also the only credible option to pursue.

It cannot be overemphasized how enveloping this approach has become in contemporary Canadian society. Public consciousness and discourse on disability is suffused with the dominant assumption that societal resources can only be effectively employed through investment in curative research programs. This supposition has become so compelling that it is now commonly regarded as a matter of "common sense," and alternative agendas of intervention are routinely discarded as undeserving of serious consideration.

There are a number of problems with this approach. First there is the purely practical difficulty of discovering a remedial solution to many categories of disability. While the benefits of medical research cannot be discounted, an exclusive emphasis on providing a cure essentially discounts the immediate, day-to-day reality of the people with disabilities. The tangible and concrete problems of everyday life cannot be deferred in anticipation of a practicable cure in the undetermined future.

Another difficulty is found in the fact that the needs and objectives of economically driven medical research programs may not coincide with the needs and objectives of members of the disabled community. No matter how well-intentioned research programs are, they frequently fail to recognize the practical priorities of disabled individuals. This state of affairs is exacerbated by the fact that the goals of research programs are as a rule controlled and directed by the non-disabled. To date, however, little attention has been given to the absence of the disabled from the kinds of medical decision-making processes that most immediately affect their own lives. In contrast, it is not difficult to imagine the extent of public outcry if, for example, Caucasian Canadians were allocated sole authority for deciding the social and economic well-being of Aboriginal communities.

But people with disabilities are not only excluded from the realm of medical decision making. The problem, in reality, is more insidious and reaches deep into the domain of Canadian society itself. Briefly stated, Canadian society is infused with an insidious "able-ism" that sustains and accentuates a view of the disabled as individuals inherently incapable of applying themselves to either the practical tasks of everyday life, or more generally, of adhering to the standards and principles that define social worth and cultural significance in Canadian society. Physical disability is not considered for what it is: a difference in the state of the body. Rather it is viewed as a sign that the individual is not a fully functioning, autonomous self, not completely a character capable of exercising freedom of choice in the pursuit of personal responsibility and self-determination.

The refusal to recognize the integrity of the disabled self finds concomitant expression in condescending attitudes of "pity" and "sympathy" and the belief that (like the very young and the very old) the disabled must be "looked after for their own good." This fundamental lack of respect for the self not only engenders forms of marginalization for the disabled but, moreover, in a cruel reversal, serves to internalize the message of exclusion to the disabled themselves. By minimizing their own expectations for equality and dignity, contemporary society effectively underlines the inequity and discrimination people with disabilities are trying to overcome.

Accessing Justice Through the Administration of Justice

Our system of justice does not always treat persons with disabilities impartially, whether the disabled individual is a victim, a witness, or the alleged perpetrator of a crime.

Estimates show that people with disabilities are four to ten times more likely to be victimized than people without disabilities. Victims with disabilities suffer repeatedly because so few of the crimes against them are reported. Caregivers often do not believe them when they do report abuse, turning people with disabilities into easy targets for predators. In some cases, the caregiver is the abuser. When a disabled person is wholly dependent upon their caregiver for the basic necessities of life, such abuse may not be reported to police at all.

Support programs for victims of crime are largely inaccessible to people with disabilities. People with disabilities who live in group homes or nursing homes are segregated from the rest of the community and its support network.

Persons with developmental/cognitive impairments and those with psychiatric disabilities are the groups most over-represented as offenders in the criminal justice system, and there are numerous systemic issues affecting the delivery of justice to persons with these disabilities.

One of the critical policy issues for persons with disabilities, beyond issues of accessibility, is access to justice. Individuals with disabilities, especially those with psychiatric disabilities, often find themselves experiencing first-hand, ineffective enforcement, prosecution, and administration of justice in Canada It is a system that is made all too often for the many and not the few. This can result in people with a mental illness facing complicated criminal trials for something as simple yet fundamental as miscommunication with police officers, lawyers, or judges.

Consider the following examples, which in actuality are loosely based on real individuals whose names have been changed:

"Sarah" has been in treatment for bipolar (manic-depressive) disorder for much of her adult life and relies on disability benefits to support herself and her children. Her mother frequently takes in the children because Sarah has been in and out of hospital for surgical and chemotherapy treatment of colon cancer.

While Sarah is very ill in the ICU, her mother dies unexpectedly, and a hostile neighbour accuses Sarah of welfare fraud. A summons is issued for her to appear in court. Sarah, who is in no physical condition to leave the hospital, and is in a fragile emotional state, misses her scheduled court appearance, and a warrant is issued for her arrest. Hospital protocol requires that the social worker notify the police of her whereabouts, and upon discharge a few weeks later, 104-pound Sarah is met by two burly police officers, handcuffed in the hospital corridor, and taken to jail.

During the course of her chemotherapy, Sarah was unable to take her prescribed psychotropic medications. While she has a prescription ready to fill, the district jail will not allow inmates to take any "mind-altering" drug. Sarah's behaviour, when she finally appears before the judge, is erratic and deemed to be disruptive. The original charge of welfare fraud is eventually dropped, but Sarah spends 45 days in jail for what she bitterly calls being sick.

"Leah" is an Aboriginal Canadian woman with a known childhood history of physical and sexual abuse. When first institutionalized, she spoke of having visions and was diagnosed with schizophrenia. The medications prescribed for her cause drowsiness, but frightening flashbacks to childhood trauma require the nurses to sedate and restrain her in a side room to prevent self-inflicted damage. Leah wakes hours later to find a man fondling her and masturbating. Her cries for help are weak, but the man flees. When Leah complains to staff about the assault, she is openly laughed at, and her story dismissed. The incident is never reported to the police, and for days afterward, Leah overhears staff joking to one another that "Leah finally got it on."

"Shaun," 20, diagnosed with schizophrenia, depression and bipolar disorder, has been in and out of jails and hospitals. Recently arrested after punching a security guard who stopped him for shoplifting an ice cream sandwich, Shaun slashed himself 150 times with a broken safety razor. When he hurts himself, the correctional officers lock him in the medical observation cell where, he says, "All I do is cry, punch myself in the face, and bang my head against the wall. There is not a day that I don't think of killing myself," he reports. "I just want help. I want this to end. I've come to the conclusion that death is the only way out."

Cognitive Impairment

As people with cognitive impairments move into the community, their likelihood of becoming involved in the criminal justice system as victims, witnesses, or suspects in a crime increases dramatically. Persons with cognitive impairments are frequently used by criminals to assist in law-breaking activities without understanding their involvement in the crime or the consequences of their involvement. Many have a profound need to be accepted and may agree to help with criminal activities in order to gain friendship. Failure to understand legal/criminal words and protocols increase their vulnerability to arrest and incarceration, even if they committed no crime. During contact with police, a person with a cognitive impairment may:

- Not want his or her disability to be recognized, and try to cover it up;
- Not understand his or her rights, but pretend to understand;
- Not understand commands;

- Be overwhelmed by police presence;
- Act upset at being detained and/or try to run away;
- Say what he or she thinks others want to hear;
- Have difficulty describing facts or details of an offence;
- Be the first to leave the scene of the crime, and the first to get caught; and
- Be confused about who is responsible for the crime and "confess" even though innocent.

Police officers often receive little or no training in the area of cognitive disability and have difficulty recognizing a person who has a cognitive impairment. Officers may interpret the person's condition as evidence of intoxication, illicit drug use, or as mental illness. Court officials face the same dilemma. Attorneys may represent individuals with cognitive impairments without realizing a disability exists. Judges may impose sentences without taking this disability into account.

Crimes against people with cognitive impairments are often labelled as abuse and neglect, which understates the criminal nature of the problem. Many victims with cognitive disabilities do not report these crimes because of dependence on the abuser for basic survival needs. When victims do report abuse, police and court officials may not take the person's allegations seriously.

Mental Illness

Large numbers of people with mental illnesses are in jails and prisons today. Police are frustrated by repeated encounters with individuals who are clearly in need of care for mental health issues, who are deemed not sufficiently ill to warrant in-patient treatment, but for whom community programs and services are also unavailable. Police officers are exasperated by the time required to turn over custody of such individuals to assessment/treatment facilities, time that takes them away from other duties—particularly when they see the same person causing the same disturbance over and over again.

Correctional officers have grown frustrated by the peculiar and sometimes dangerous behaviours exhibited by mentally ill offenders in their facilities. They are concerned for the safety of their staff and other inmates, as well as the mentally ill offender. Most recognize that these inmates need help, not punishment, but the human and financial resources required to provide treatment are often unavailable.

The unmet social and health needs of people with serious mental illnesses increasingly spiral out of control in a vicious pattern of recidivism. Communities across Canada and the Western world are endeavouring to address these problems through collaborative efforts that span the boundaries of mental health and criminal justice and also cross the different phases of justice system involvement, such as pre-arrest diversion, court diversion, programs/services within detention facilities that target the behaviours leading to incarceration, and case management approaches to reintegration and discharge planning.

Unfortunately, problems in the administration of justice reflect discrimination within the justice system itself. The inequality present in society is sometimes reflected in the judicial system, where persons with cognitive and/or psychiatric disabilities experience no general attitude of equality, but only a right to equal protection under the law.

The protection of all persons must start at the stage of first contact with the police, and law enforcement officers need to be trained to ask questions that will de-escalate a crisis and elicit a history of mental illness or other disability so that the right supports can be provided to assist the accused. Those who lack the financial resources to ensure their defence, but do not meet the stringent eligibility criteria of legal aid, are too easily denied due process of law. And when marginalized persons are incarcerated without the opportunity to address the behaviours that led to their incarceration, and are subsequently discharged into the community without a source of income, housing, transportation, education, or hope for gainful employment, they have little choice but to re-offend. Without the means to identify and treat individuals with special needs, the revolving door will never be stilled.

Institutionalized discrimination largely results from a failure to take action to address discrimination. A society that espouses dignity for all its citizens must examine how and why cases are brought to the court and how they are dealt with, and look closely at the social support systems that currently are failing large numbers of people.

⌇

CHAPTER 4

Dignity in the Community

*If you prick us, do we not bleed? if you tickle us, do we not laugh? if you
poison us, do we not die? and if you wrong us, shall we not revenge?*
William Shakespeare from *Merchant of Venice*, Act III, Scene I

COMMUNITY ISSUES FOR PWDS go far beyond the need for ramps and
accessible transportation. While most able-bodied people take home and workplaces for granted, even these basics of "normal life" can provide unexpected and
unnecessary barriers. A detailed case study of how, in the absence of support
systems based on Independent Living (IL) principles, a former client of mine
quite tragically fell through the cracks will illustrate some of the barriers most
people do not see. It will become obvious that the principles of Independent
Living are critical to achieving an equal and inclusive Canadian society.

Independent Living in Canada

The lead non-governmental response to redressing historical wrongs that have
marginalized persons with a disability is the Independent Living movement.
The IL movement in Canada is part of a broad international approach to disability issues that promotes autonomy, control, and flexibility. Many Canadian
non-governmental organizations have adopted these principles as core tenets of
their development, with the Canadian Association of Independent Living
Centres (CAILC) providing an organizational infrastructure to advance this
important perspective.

CAILC is a national umbrella organization, representing and coordinating the network of Independent Living Resource Centres [ILRCs] at the national level. Through this consumer-driven network, CAILC provides services annually to over 250,000 persons with a disability. CAILC is a national, bilingual, non-profit organization, and is governed by a board of directors comprised of a majority of people with disabilities.

CAILC promotes a Canada where rights and responsibilities are shared between citizens and the state, focusing on building a country based on the principles of inclusion, equity, affordability, and justice. While the aim of IL is not to make a person "normal" in a physical or mental sense, the movement emphasizes the value of people with disabilities to have ordinary life experiences by providing community-based, consumer-controlled services, supports, resources, and skills training to enable people with disabilities to live an "ordinary life" in the community.

This multi-faceted approach to greater inclusion and participation of persons with a disability has created benefits at all economic, social, political, and cultural levels within Canada.

The Canadian Association for Community Living, and similar disability empowerment groups, promote the perspective that persons with a disability will gain maximum autonomy and self-actualization when they are allowed to direct their own service needs in a barrier-free environment. The IL philosophy takes a holistic, cross-disability approach, addressing the full continuum of needs faced by persons with a disability. As CAILC notes:

Independent Living (IL) is a social movement of, for, and by people with disabilities. It is guided by the principle that in our society all citizens have the right and duty to take responsibility for their own lives. This sense of self-direction and self-actualization is embodied in all aspects of the IL movement in the belief that developing independence means overcoming dependency. The movement promotes human rights, deinstitutionalization, and full and equal participation for all in the community and in society.

A central goal of the IL movement is the removal of social and environmental barriers that prevent persons with disabilities from controlling their own lives. In part, the IL model is an alternative social model to the medical service delivery approach. Rather than searching for a cure to a particular condition, people with disabilities are provided with the knowledge and skills to explore options, make choices, take risks, and make their own mistakes as they themselves decide on a course of action for their daily lives. People with disabilities must be empowered to participate fully in their society and community and must be able to direct and manage their own resources, from home support and transportation to education, health care, and human rights. In short, IL is founded on the right of people with disabilities to:

- live with dignity in their chosen community;
- participate in all aspects of their life; and
- control and make decisions about their own lives.

To achieve these objectives, Independent Living Resource Centres have been built across Canada. These centres are "disability-led, cross-disability focused, community-based, and committed to the full citizenship of all Canadians with disabilities, regardless of disability." In addition, people with disabilities hold the majority of staff and board positions. These centres offer the following core programs:

- **Information and Networking**—providing clear and up-to-date information on resources and options accessible to everyone, and promoting IL to PWDs, their families, friends, community and support networks, and to government;
- **Individualized Self-Advocacy and Skills Development**—offering opportunities for self-help, learning skills, personal growth, individual empowerment, dealing with barriers and discrimination, and taking control of their lives;
- **Peer Support**—sharing knowledge from life experience, developing leadership skills, reducing individual isolation, and supporting rights and responsibilities;
- **Research and Development**—identifying gaps in service, creating new options, and demonstrating the IL model of service delivery.

They further suggest adopting an "independent living lens" when developing programs or policies. In order to test whether this approach has been taken, CAILC poses the following questions:

- Does the program/policy support the IL philosophy/model? Does it take a holistic personalized approach that focuses on individual needs rather than institutional interests?

- Does it uphold the principles of control, choice, and flexibility?
- Does it support full citizenship?
- Is the information accessible? Is it available in a variety of formats?
- Does it involve people with disabilities through consultation and collaboration?

With centres now across Canada, the United States, and parts of Russia the principles appear flexible enough to provide culturally appropriate services, and a strong network has emerged to benefit persons with a disability.

Creating an Accommodating Workplace

Simply providing equality or freedom from discrimination is indeed not enough, as many court cases have shown over the years. For example, an individual who uses a wheelchair may be able to apply for a job in the same way that an able-bodied person would; however, if there is no ramp and automatic doors where the interview is to take place then they are clearly disadvantaged. To answer this apparent gap, legislatures and courts have developed the duty to accommodate. The concept is straightforward: Every reasonable effort, short of undue hardship, must be made to accommodate a person with a disability.

In practical terms, what does accommodation look like? This is a particularly pertinent question when examining equality in the workplace. In order to develop a policy that promotes independence for the employee so that she or he avoids barriers, and more fully integrates in the workplace, several groups suggest adopting an "independent living lens," as outlined previously. While not exhaustive, those questions may be a helpful guide in developing a welcoming environment for the disabled employee, and meeting "duty to accommodate" standards.

In addition to considering a legal duty for the employer to accommodate, it is also critical to understand the context in which such a policy must be constructed. First, disabled employees are on the vanguard of reversing a legacy of discrimination and socio-economic barriers. Second, disability is a personal characteristic, and as such should not be a barrier to equal treatment. Third, any rule or policy must be premised upon promoting the dignity of the disabled employee. Fourth, a disabled employee has already signed an employment contract from which accommodation costs arise. Finally, it is important to appreciate that disabled employees want the same as their able-bodied co-workers—respect and recognition for their efforts, collegiality in the workplace, and an absence of barriers that highlight differences rather than commonalities.

A policy of accommodation should appreciate the above factors. However, employers all too often do not include the disabled employee in the development of such policies. This limits choice, creates low morale, and is shortsighted. Not only do disabled employees have the right to earn a living like their able-bodied colleagues, they have much to contribute to their employers.

Community Supports for Independent Living

Community care supports and funding for self-directed care have made institutionalized living a thing of the past for most people with quadriplegia. This brave new world of autonomy, however, deteriorates when intersected with a psychiatric disability. A person with quadriplegia will not only encounter a double disability, but a new level of discrimination with arising social barriers, an abrogation of autonomy through systemic controls applied by medical practitioners and mental health professionals, and a lack of community supports capable of providing for individual needs. This is further complicated by a lack of communication between the attending psychiatrist and the rehabilitation team.

Several studies indicate that 25 to 45 percent of persons with a spinal cord injury (SCI) experience depression, while other studies suggest that a considerable percentage have a personality disorder.[8] Therefore, it may be reasonable to conclude that a significant number of persons with SCI will need mental health support and/or intervention. While it is clear that a minority of these persons will require hospitalization for a psychiatric disorder, these numbers may also be meaningful.

A client of mine, whom we will call "Joseph Janowski" (not his real name) encountered housing and legal problems that forced him to reside in a psychiatric hospital even after his mental health had stabilized and he was ready to

---

8.   H. Livneh and R. Antonak, *Psychosocial Adaptation to Chronic Illness and Disability* (Maryland, Aspen Publishers, 1997).

reside in the community again. The psychosocial barriers that he encountered, in the end, remained insurmountable due to a lack of cross-training between the physical and mental health support communities.

Client Background and Problem Summary

Joseph Janowski was a 57-year-old single male who was born in Eastern Europe. He came to Canada in 1961 and became a landed immigrant. When he was 18, he suffered a spinal cord injury requiring him to rely on a wheelchair. He had also been diagnosed with schizo-affective disorder or bipolar-affective disorder.

Mr. Janowski had a history of public disturbances arising from his psychiatric disorder(s). In 1995, he had caused $8,000 damage to his subsidized apartment, and after a brief period of institutionalization, he was advised that he could not return to the apartment until he paid for the damages. In 1997, he found alternative accommodation with a personal care service provision agency. By 1999, he had paid more than half of the cost of damages caused in 1995. This difficulty in finding accommodation and consequent financial hardship substantially increased the psychosocial barriers confronting him.

In July 1998, Mr. Janowski was again admitted to a psychiatric facility. At the time, he was described as unkempt, dirty, and malodorous. His medical chart indicated that he was angry and threatening, and his thought form tangential. While Mr. Janowski would periodically appear highly intellectual and astute, he also frequently suffered delusions of persecution. Initially, during this stay in the hospital, his psychiatrist made a decision that he was incapable of consenting to his own treatment. In August 1998, the Consent and Capacity Review Board, after reviewing the evidence, found that Mr. Janowski was capable of consenting to his own treatment. He was then free to go home. Unfortunately, he had no home to which he could go. Because he did not have wheelchair-accessible housing, he did not leave the hospital until October 2001, more than three years later.

After attempting to live in the community without any support systems, Mr. Janowski was again admitted to hospital in January 2002. His physician subsequently made a determination that he was incapable to consent to his own treatment. Mr. Janowski was trapped in an impossible cycle of insensitivity and prejudice. Further community options were explored, but there was no accessible supportive housing available for persons with both a psychiatric and significant physical disability. Personal care service providers were reluctant to take him on as a client because of his mental health history. Mental health intervention may have decreased these problems prior to hospitalization, but the community mental health workers did not want to provide the physical care necessary for a client who used a wheelchair. Potential agencies that could provide the physical care were partly trapped by their own negative stereotypes of persons with a psychiatric disability, and their training did not include how to respond to an individual who had occasional bouts of irrational thinking. He was therefore forced to remain in the psychiatric facility, despite the fact that this was unnecessary.

The Legal Problem and Strategy

Mr. Janowski's landlord was an agency that provided attendant care services for persons with a disability. While he was in hospital, although there was a lease in place and no notice was given, the landlord rented his apartment to another individual. Clearly, the landlord wanted to be rid of him because of problems related to his psychiatric disability. If he could not return home with additional mental health support, then he would have to stay in hospital. Since the psychiatrist was not creating a barrier to him being discharged, we felt the only legal recourse was to pursue a wrongful eviction and let the caregivers improve their training as a matter of their contractual obligation. Mr. Janowski was not the problem, the support systems were the problem and that had to be emphasized.

A complaint was then filed with the Ontario Rental Housing Tribunal for wrongful eviction. It was decided that negotiation and/or mediation was the first necessary step because Mr. Janowski would need an ongoing relationship with the landlord/care provider. Therefore, a "mutual interest" approach to negotiation was undertaken. Initially, the landlord appeared sensitive to the client's needs, but he did not want the client to return to his apartments because of past damage to the premises.

The landlord was aware that the client was serious about the appeal, and did undertake to find other housing. However, a successful complaint would win the battle but lose the war. The landlord had not charged the client for the extensive damage that he had caused prior to his second admission to the psychiatric facility, but indicated that if the tribunal allowed Mr. Janowski to return to his apartment, he would be billed several thousand dollars for repairs. Therefore, we had a standoff.

The objective for the client remained to find suitable housing. Rather than proceed to the finality of a tribunal hearing, and with this lose our leverage in negotiating, and furthermore leave my client with overwhelming damages, we attempted settlement.

We were aware that, in addition to Mr. Janowski's immediate housing needs, it was necessary to get him out of the cycle that brought him to the psychiatric hospital for periodic readmission. He needed appropriate personal care. We believed that if his mental health support and/or personal care assistants had intervened in a proactive way to guard against his decline in mental health, then admission to the psychiatric hospital might have been prevented. However, the attendants were average care providers with no background or expertise in mental health, and the mental health support workers had little or no appreciation for the physical care that this gentleman needed.

Meeting the objective required a delicate balancing of appropriate housing with sensitive and knowledgeable care providers. An agreement was reached with the landlord and the care provider that attempted to meet the client's needs. The settlement was drafted as follows:

1. The client withdraws his complaint against the landlord with respect to wrongful termination of his tenancy at the subsidized residence. Both parties also withdraw any future claims for damages that may have arisen from the above-mentioned tenancy.

2. The landlord will assist the client in finding accommodation and providing personal support services in the community of Thunder Bay, Ontario, and, in particular, at a building in Thunder Bay, Ontario, that is owned by the psychiatric hospital.

3. The personal support services provided to the client by the landlord are to include the following:
    (a) The landlord will act as agent for delivering arranged support funded by [another agency];

(b) The landlord will hire only male support care workers who have experience with individuals who have a psychiatric disability;

(c) The landlord will provide support care workers with the consent of the client;

(d) Both parties will be bound by a service agreement to be negotiated at a future date.

4. The client will designate an individual to coordinate communication and/or a case conference of all individuals and/or organizations responsible for community-based support services for the client's daily living activities.

5. In the event that a dispute arises between the client and the landlord that cannot be resolved within the normal administrative channels, a mediator will be appointed at the consent of both parties to address the matter.

Postscript

After experiencing the stress of several months in a psychiatric hospital without cause, Joseph Janowski chose to stop taking his medication and his mental health declined significantly. In the 1960s, Mr. Janowski had lived in Eastern Europe under a totalitarian government, and he often said that the hospital was worse than a communist state. One may infer the tremendous strain and hopelessness that he must have felt, and wonder if this had an impact on his decision to refuse treatment. Despite the efforts of several parties, no community-based housing has been found for this individual. He presently remains in a psychiatric facility.

In fact, as the months passed and he refused treatment, although he was not a danger to himself or others, a physician again certified him as incapable of consenting to his own treatment. This means that now the doctor can administer any medication that he or she wishes. The patient must be found incapable of understanding the information given to him or her with respect to treatment, and be incapable of appreciating the consequences of lack of treatment.

Mr. Janowski appealed the decision of the physician to the Consent and Capacity Review Board, but failed. As an additional concern the Consent and Capacity Review Board failed to recognize that he could appreciate the consequences of a decision or lack of decision, as a result of a narrow interpretation of the facts and/or stereotyping of wheelchair users with a spinal cord injury. In particular, the board allowed patronizing statements respecting wheelchair users to be believed, and in their reasons focused too closely on the possibility of weight gain due to proposed psychiatric medications affecting his mobility. As a result, the board ignored the fact that the patient indicated that with his activity level he was unlikely to gain weight. The board further failed to consider the fact that the appellant's personal and religious convictions against medication combined with his past horrific experiences with prescribed anti-psychotic medication was of paramount concern when refusing the physician's proposed medical protocol. He did not bother to appeal the board's decision.

Recommendations

I will always regret the outcome of this case, and wish that I could have done something different to better assist this vulnerable man. The systemic barriers were just too entrenched against him. I did, however, learn a great deal from these failures, and realized the following recommendations, if followed, would have been a tremendous help to him, and all other persons who have both a psychiatric and physical disability. These are:

- Community-based housing for persons with a psychiatric disability should be wheelchair accessible;
- Sensitivity training and knowledge of psychiatric disability should be made a part of orientation and learning for personal care assistants;
- Litigation should be considered for persons with physical and psychiatric disabilities who cannot access community support;
- Agency care providers and/or landlords who assist persons with a physical disability should also adopt support for persons with a psychiatric disability within their mandate and mission;
- Funding for community-based housing that can meet the needs of persons with a physical and psychiatric disability should be increased;
- More study into the subject area is needed, so that a comprehensive policy regarding the dilemma facing persons with both a psychiatric and physical disability may be devised;

- Future policy and accommodation options should be devised from the perspective of the PWD, so that individuals and organizations representing users of psychiatric and physical disability services play a leading role in its development.

Accommodation in workplaces, social programs, housing, and the community in general, benefit us all in the long-run.

❧

CHAPTER 5

Dignity in Law

When I walked out of prison, that was my mission, to liberate the oppressed and the oppressor both. Some say that has now been achieved. But I know that that is not the case. The truth is that we are not yet free; we have merely achieved the freedom to be free, the right not to be oppressed. We have not taken the final step of our journey, but the first step on a longer and even more difficult road. For to be free is not merely to cast off one's chains, but to live in a way that respects and enhances the freedom of others. The true test of our devotion to freedom is just beginning.

Nelson Mandela, from *A Long Walk to Freedom*

THE CENTRAL CONCEPT TO LEGAL ADVANCEMENT for persons with a disability is "equality," and within its rubric the ancillary term "duty to accommodate." Arguably, recent decisions of courts and tribunals have interpreted and applied these legal principles in a manner that makes dignity in the law currently the most progressive of the Six Degrees model. The approach to equality taken by the Supreme Court of Canada, and the critical role that the duty to accommodate has played in promoting a more inclusive Canada, shows that while the law is a powerful tool, it also has its limitations. It would be pure folly to rely exclusively on pronouncements from the Supreme Court to achieve full equality for persons with a disability while ignoring the dynamic opportunities guaranteed by incorporating the other five degrees of dignity.

Duty to Accommodate

The courts found that simply providing equality or freedom from discrimination was indeed not enough and thus the idea of the "duty to accommodate" has been developed: Every reasonable effort, short of undue hardship, must be made to accommodate a person with a disability. The duty to accommodate is prescribed in both the *Ontario Human Rights Code* (OHRC) and the *Canadian Human Rights Act* (CHRA). The OHRC states:

17. (1) Disability—A right of a person under this Act is not infringed for the reason only that the person is incapable of performing or fulfilling the essential duties or requirements attending the exercise of the right because of disability.

(2) Accommodation—The commission, the Tribunal or a court shall not find a person incapable unless it is satisfied that the needs of the person cannot be accommodated without undue hardship on the person responsible for accommodating those needs, considering the cost, outside sources of funding, if any, and health and safety requirements, if any.

And the CHRA states:

3. (1) For all purposes of this Act, the prohibited grounds of discrimination are race, national or ethnic origin, colour, religion, age, sex, sexual orientation, marital status, family status, disability, and conviction for which a pardon has been granted.

15. (1) It is not a discriminatory practice if:

(*a*) any refusal, exclusion, expulsion, suspension, limitation, specification or preference in relation to any employment is established by an employer to be based on a bona fide occupational requirement;

(*g*) in the circumstances described in section 5 or 6, an individual is denied any goods, services, facilities or accommodation or access thereto or occupancy of any commercial premises or residential accommodation or is a victim of any adverse differentiation and there is bona fide justification for that denial or differentiation.

(2) For any practice mentioned in paragraph (1) (a) to be considered to be based on a bona fide occupational requirement and for any practice

mentioned in paragraph (1) (g) to be considered to have a bona fide justification, it must be established that accommodation of the needs of an
individual or a class of individuals affected would impose undue hardship
on the person who would have to accommodate those needs, considering
health, safety and cost.

The Supreme Court of Canada adopted what is termed the Meiorin test in
two seminal cases—Meiorin and Grismer—dealing with the parameters surrounding the duty to accommodate and the defence of bona fide occupational
requirement (BFOR).

The Meiorin Decision[9]

Tawney Meiorin was a female forest fighter who had been dismissed from her
job because she failed one aspect of a minimum fitness standard established by
the Government of British Columbia for all firefighters. After Ms. Meiorin had
been performing the duties of a firefighter for three years, the government
adopted a new series of fitness tests, including a running test designed to measure aerobic fitness. After failing the test and losing her job, Ms. Meiorin com-
plained that because women generally have lower aerobic capacity, the aerobic
standard discriminated against women in contravention of the British
Columbia Human Rights Code.

The Government of British Columbia argued that this standard was a
BFOR of the firefighter position, although they could not demonstrate that
the expert they had employed from the University of Victoria had established
its guidelines for the fitness test on a rational connection to the job itself. The
expert had to admit that his model was, in fact, arbitrary. On appeal, the
Supreme Court determined that the standard was not a BFOR. The Court's
rationale, dealing in part with the issue of direct versus adverse effect discrimination, was as follows:

- It is sometimes difficult to characterize discrimination accurately as having either a direct or adverse effect. In some circumstances, it allows the
  discriminator to choose an adverse effect form for the discrimination to

---

9. *British Columbia (Public Service Employee Relations Commission) v. British Columbia Government and Service
    Employees' Union [1999] 3 S.C.R. 3.*

avoid the harsher consequences of a finding of direct discrimination;

- The approach provides different outcomes depending on the characterization, e.g., the policy or standard may be struck down in its entirety if the BFOR is not established, whereas under the indirect test, the policy or standard remains intact as long as the employer can establish the rational connection requirement, and the focus shifts to individual accommodation;

- The approach is premised on an incorrect assumption that the adversely affected group is a minority by allowing a policy or standard to be left in place if it only affects a small group. This leaves the size of the group affected open to manipulation and is unhelpful where the group is, in fact, the majority;

- There are difficulties with the practical application of the defences. For example, under the direct test the employer is forced to consider reasonable alternatives to the standard whereas under the adverse effect test there is no such requirement;

- The approach legitimizes systemic discrimination since policies or standards that appear neutral, in that they are applied equally to everyone, are not themselves challenged and tribunals and courts cannot assess their legitimacy;

- The approach is inconsistent with both the purpose and terms of human rights legislation, to which a purposive and liberal interpretation is given, and the actual terms of the legislation. There is no distinction between direct and adverse effect discrimination in specific provisions of human rights legislation nor is the duty to accommodate linked legislatively with adverse effect discrimination;

- The approach creates a dissonance between human rights legislation and analysis based on the Charter or Rights and Freedoms, since the Charter gives "little legal importance" to the distinction.

Furthermore, the Court indicated that the duty to accommodate imposes a primary obligation to systemically remove the sources of discrimination. In outlining the duty to accommodate, Justice McLaughlin wrote:

Having considered the various alternatives, I propose the following three-step test for determining whether a prima facie discriminatory standard is a BFOR. An employer may justify the impugned standard by establishing on the balance of probabilities:

1. that the employer adopted the standard for a purpose rationally connected to the performance of the job;

2. that the employer adopted the particular standard in an honest and good faith belief that it was necessary to the fulfillment of that legitimate work-related purpose; and

3. that the standard is reasonably necessary to the accomplishment of that legitimate work-related purpose. To show that the standard is reasonably necessary, it must be demonstrated that it is impossible to accommodate individual employees sharing the characteristics of the claimant without imposing undue hardship upon the employer.[10]

The Grismer Decision[11]

Three months after the Meiorin decision, the Court gave its decision in Grismer, a case in which the respondent raised a bona fide justification (BFJ) defence. Terry Grismer had a condition known as homonymous hemianopia (HH), which eliminated his left-side peripheral vision in both eyes. The British Columbia Superintendent of Motor Vehicles cancelled his driver's license on the ground that his vision no longer met the standard of a minimum field of vision of 120 degrees. People with HH were never permitted to drive.

Mr. Grismer reapplied several times, passing the entire requisite tests except the field of vision test, and was not permitted to demonstrate that he was able to compensate for his limited field of vision. He therefore filed a complaint with the British Columbia Council of Human Rights and was successful at tribunal on the basis that the superintendent had failed to prove that there was a BFJ for the rigid standard applied to people with HH.

On appeal, the Supreme Court of Canada made it clear that the approach set out in Meiorin is equally applicable in service provision cases. It applied the same approach to this complaint, which had been filed many years before the Meiorin

---

10. *Ibid,* paragraph 54.
11. British Columbia (Superintendent of Motor Vehicles) v. British Columbia (Council of Human Rights) [1999] 3 S.C.R. 868.

Six Degrees of Dignity: Disability in an Age of Freedom

decision. It concluded that the 120-degree vision standard was not reasonably necessary, and the standard was struck down. In writing the court's decision on Grismer, Justice McLaughlin further described the duty to accommodate:

> "Accommodation" refers to what is required in the circumstances to avoid discrimination. Standards must be as inclusive as possible... There is more than one way to establish that the necessary level of accommodation has not been provided. In Meiorin, the government failed to demonstrate that its standard was sufficiently accommodating, because it failed to adduce evidence linking the standard (a certain aerobic capacity) to the purpose (safety and efficiency in fire fighting). In Mr. Grismer's case, a general connection has been established between the standard (a certain field of peripheral vision) and the purpose or goal of reasonable highway safety. However, the appellant argues that some drivers with less than the stipulated field of peripheral vision can drive safely and that the standard is discriminatory because it does not provide for individualized assessment. Failure to accommodate may be established by evidence of arbitrariness in setting the standard, by an unreasonable refusal to provide individual assessment, or perhaps in some other way. The ultimate issue is whether the employer or service provider has shown that it provides accommodation to the point of undue hardship.[12]

The Court held that discriminatory barriers to equality were to be modified and made "as inclusive as possible," so that systemic discrimination is not perpetuated. The onus for demonstrating that making the most inclusive accommodation would cause "undue hardship" is on the respondent. In Meiorin, the Supreme Court recognized that made it clear that once a prima facie case of discrimination was established, the actual source of the discrimination was to be eliminated according to a unified discrimination analysis. As a consequence, systemic change was to occur unless making the change would cause undue hardship. As recognized in Grismer, if this approach were not adopted the source of the discrimination would remain in place and continue to "exclude those not prepared to challenge it or demand accommodation." [A note to readers: An excellent discussion of both the Meiorin and Grismer decisions can be found on the Canadian Human Rights Commission website: www.chrc-ccdp.ca.]

---

12. *Ibid*, paragraph 22.

Canadian Charter of Rights and Freedoms

While the duty to accommodate and the removal of the distinction between direct and indirect discrimination are wonderful progress toward equality for PWDs, it is not a panacea, nor does it allow unfettered claims of discrimination. According to human rights principles, once a complainant has disclosed the need for accommodation, the responsibility for devising the accommodation devolves upon the party in the best position to determine how the complainant can be accommodated: the respondent. There is no question but that the burden of proving accommodation of "factors relating to the unique capabilities and inherent worth and dignity of every individual, up to the point of undue hardship" rests likewise on the respondent. This creates a conundrum whereby the Supreme Court has invoked a "reasonableness" standard into a section 15 analysis, although this approach was earlier rejected. As the Supreme Court stated in Eldridge:

> The obligation to make reasonable accommodation for those adversely affected by a facially neutral policy or rule extends only to the point of "undue hardship." In my view, in s. 15(1) cases this principle is best addressed as a component of the s. 1 analysis. Reasonable accommodation, in this context, is generally equivalent to the concept of "reasonable limits." It should not be employed to restrict the ambit of s. 15(1).[13]

To address this apparent inconsistency, the Court should apply the test for "undue hardship" under a section 1 analysis, should it find that there is a prima facie breach of section 15. Section 1 reads:

> The Canadian Charter of Rights and Freedoms guarantees the rights and freedoms set out in it subject only to such reasonable limits prescribed by law as can be demonstrably justified in a free and democratic society.

As the terms of the section make clear, no Charter protection is absolute. In the presence of a section 15 violation, the courts therefore undertake a separate section 1 evaluation to determine whether the infringement nevertheless constitutes a reasonable limit to the equality rights guarantee.

The government bears the burden of establishing that any Charter breach

---

13. *Eldridge v. British Columbia (Attorney General)* [1997] 3S.C.R. 624, 1997 115 CAN 327 (C.S.C.).

is justified. The governing approach to section 1 analysis detailed by the Supreme Court of Canada in *R. v. Oakes*[14] involves a two-step process. First, the objective of the legislation or government action must be shown to be sufficiently "pressing and substantial" to warrant overriding a Charter right. Second, the means adopted to attain that objective must be reasonable and demonstrably justified. This step entails a proportionality test in which the courts are required "to balance the interests of society with those of individuals or groups." Three elements must be satisfied:

1. The measures adopted must be rationally connected to the objective;

2. The measures adopted should cause minimal impairment to the right or freedom in question; and

3. There must be proportionality between the effects of the measures limiting the right or freedom and the objective identified as being sufficiently important, and between the deleterious and salutary effects of the measures at issue.

In the years since Oakes, the application of its "strict" section 1 test has undergone adjustments. In particular, the Supreme Court of Canada has developed a flexible approach to the Oakes test's "minimal impairment" requirement that has resulted in a less stringent section 1 analysis in certain cases.[15]

Section 1 has also recently been used in *Auton et al v. British Columbia*[16] where the parents of autistic children wanted intensive and effective, but expensive treatment for their children. The Supreme Court of Canada found that health care funding was a matter of provincial jurisdiction and the British Columbia Government could essentially fund treatments that it felt necessary without discriminating against these children with autism. As the Court noted:

The legislative scheme is not itself discriminatory in providing funding for

---

14. *[1986] 1 S.C.R. 103.*

15. *Dagenais v. Canadian Broadcasting Corp., [1994] 3 S.C.R. 835,* at 889; *Irwin Toy Ltd. v. Quebec (A.G.), [1989] 1 S.C.R. 927* (provincial regulation limiting advertising directed to children); *Slaight Communications Inc. v. Davidson, [1989] 1 S.C.R. 1038* (adjudicator's order requiring employer to provide positive letter of reference to wrongfully dismissed employee); *R. v. Keegstra, [1990] 3 S.C.R. 697* (Criminal Code provision prohibiting the dissemination of hate propaganda); *R. v. Butler, [1992] 1 S.C.R. 452* (Criminal Code provision prohibiting the dissemination of obscenity); *Little Sisters Book and Art Emporium v. Canada (Minister of Justice), [2000] 2 S.C.R. 1 1 20, 2000 SCC 69* (application of Butler "obscenity" test to gay and lesbian material); *R. v. Edwards Books and Art Ltd., [1986] 2 S.C.R. 713* (freedom of religion: retail employees); *Public Service Alliance of Canada et al. v. The Queen in tight of Canada et al., [1987] 1 S.C.R. 424* (freedom of association: workers not party to a P.S.A.C. challenge); *Rodriguez v. British Columbia (Attorney General), [1993] 3 S.C.R. 519* (security of the person: disabled persons).

16. *2004 SCC 78.*

---

non-core services to some groups while denying funding for ABA/IBI therapy to autistic children. The scheme is, by its very terms, a partial health plan and its purpose is not to meet all medical needs.

In this instance, it appears clear that the law of equality, or a Court's decision, cannot be an end in itself. It is critical to raise questions of discrimination to the political, cultural, and societal level. In other words, employ the Six Degrees.

VIA Rail v. Council of Canadians with Disabilities[17]

In 2003, VIA Rail purchased train cars from British Rail at bargain basement prices. They were inexpensive because they no longer met European accessibility standards. Before the trains were purchased, using 100 percent taxpayer money, former Liberal Transportation Minister David Collenette promised the trains would meet Canadian Transportation Agency (CTA) accessibility standards. When told the trains were inaccessible, Collenette washed his hands of the matter, suggesting VIA seek the CTA's guidance on the issue. In October 2003, the CTA ordered VIA Rail to make the cars accessible to persons with mobility and visual disabilities. VIA refused and took the case to the Federal Court of Appeal (FCA). In March 2005, the FCA overturned the CTA's decision, saying people with disabilities who can't use the new trains will have to find other means of transportation. As a result, Canada is the only developed country in the world where new inaccessible trains—comprising one-third of VIA's fleet—are being brought into service.

Can you imagine if a retailer or food outlet such as Tim Hortons or McDonald's attempted the same argument in any Canadian city? What if they made one-third of the Tim Hortons restaurants in Canada inaccessible to wheelchairs? It would be unthinkable that a wheelchair user somewhere in Canada would not launch a human rights complaint. This happened to Famous Players Theatres where they had inaccessible cinemas. The Ontario Human Rights Tribunal in *Turnbull et al v. Famous Players* (2001) ordered these movie houses closed. But in the VIA Rail decision the FCA failed to exercise similar reasoning, and be consistent with evolving Human Rights norms.

Fortunately, the Council of Canadians with Disabilities (CCD) appealed this decision to the Supreme Court of Canada, where I hope better thinking

---

17. *2005 FCA 79.*

will prevail. The case went before the Supreme Court of Canada on May 19, 2006, and is still under review.

Co-counsel Paul Claude Bérubé and I represented the Canadian Association of Independent Living Centres (CAILC), which was granted intervener status in the Supreme Court case. In an argument that was consistent with CCD and several other interveners, we submitted that the constitutional values of equality and the duty to accommodate arise from respect and understanding of the economic, social, and cultural contributions that persons with a disability make through full participation in the Canadian mosaic. VIA Rail failed to meet the test for accommodating persons with disabilities as articulated by this Court.

CAILC was aware that the Appellant and Respondent placed several procedural and substantive issues before the Court. Also, approximately twelve parties were granted intervener status. CAILC therefore wanted to narrow its focus to the following facts: First, VIA Rail purchased 139 Renaissance rail cars, notwithstanding the fact that they were inaccessible to persons who use wheelchairs and/or have other disabilities; second, the Renaissance cars represent one-third of all cars in the network. This share would increase as the old "conforming" cars age and are gradually removed from the network. CAILC also limited its argument to the following points:

ISSUE I   VIA Rail failed to ensure that it has accommodated passengers with a disability up to the point of undue financial hardship pursuant to section 15(1) of the Charter, and the denial of these rights cannot be saved by section 1 of the Charter of Rights and Freedoms;

ISSUE II   Canada is a State Party to International Human Rights Law that requires a higher standard of accessibility and accommodation than has been undertaken by VIA Rail;

ISSUE III VIA Rail has failed to apply the Canada Transportation Act in a manner consistent with its legal obligations.

The parameters of accommodation must include the same expectations and rights afforded to non-disabled members of Canadian society. For example, disabled Canadians must be afforded the same opportunities for participation—which means a service cannot be deemed "accessible" if some members of

Canadian society are relegated to only accessing a limited and inconvenient number of options from their non-disabled peers. Therefore, the Supreme Court was asked to interpret the legislation in a manner consistent with a definition of accommodation that comports with previously articulated equality principles and promotes an inclusive society through consideration and recognition of the social, cultural, and economic contributions made by disabled Canadians. We further emphasized that the above interpretation was appropriate because every enactment is deemed remedial, and shall be given such fair, large, and liberal construction and interpretation as best ensures the attainment of its objects.[18]

The FCA had misapplied the test for "undue-ness." CAILC therefore, asked the court to read into the record part of the Canadian Transportation Act, which applies a large and liberal approach to established equality principles.[19] If the Supreme Court confirmed the Federal Court of Appeal's analysis that requires taking the entire network into account, the Renaissance cars will, through attrition, come to dominate the fleet. As a result VIA Rail will be regressive in its remote assertions that it meets acceptable equality standards in the delivery of its services. In addition, a reconfiguration of the cars would be costly, but would not cross the threshold of undue financial hardship.

VIA Rail's actions therefore cannot be saved by Section 1. Indeed, it is persons with a disability and the guarantee of their equality that are critical to the success of a "free and democratic society." Their inclusion and unencumbered participation can only be viewed as a positive contribution to the Canadian mosaic, and an indicator of the health of its democracy.

VIA Rail, through its actions, attempted in a most insensitive manner to return to a "separate but equal" perspective that should have been kept in the dustbin of the pre civil rights movement of the 1960s. To allow VIA Rail to succeed in this matter will create a fabricated equality, which, under its veneer, can only end in unrelenting, purposeful, and systemic disadvantage for persons with a disability in Canada.

---

18. According to the *Interpretation Act*, R.S.C. 1985, c. I-21, Section 12, and the Supreme Courts decision in *Zurich Insurance Co. v. Ontario (Human Rights Commission)*, 2 S.C.R. 321 at 339.
19. Part V of the *Canadian Transportation Act S.C. 1996*, c. 10 (the "Act").

Conclusion

The duty to accommodate sets a high standard for a respondent to argue a winnable defence—they must prove that to accommodate would cause undue financial hardship. The respondent must not only show by way of evidence that they do not have the financial capacity to accommodate an individual with a disability, but that outside funding was sought, modifications for a person with a disability were thoroughly considered, and, in the instance of employment, alternate positions in the workplace were investigated on behalf of the disabled employee. Furthermore, the employer must demonstrate that it has made all appropriate efforts to provide a dignified work environment. The courts have arguably been very progressive, but the question remains: Do their decisions trickle down to a grassroots level to impact those who have been traditionally disempowered?

While from a disability rights perspective, the legislative and jurisprudential advancements for persons with a disability may appear quite heartening, and they create a progressive framework for the assertion of rights, the fact is that they are decided on a case-by-case basis. The law does create standards of adherence, and the duty to accommodate can cost a discriminator a great deal by way of damages if they are caught in the net of human rights complaints proceedings. It cannot, however, be assumed that wrongdoers are going to change their actions just because of a tribunal or court decision, or for that matter that they even perceive themselves as breaching human rights law. Also given that persons with a disability very often are disempowered, and that social psychologists indicate that this subordination normalizes discrimination, the question arises whether a disabled individual would wish to assert his or her rights. This coupled with the prolonged stress related to the wait for a complaint to be heard (19.9 months in Ontario for a human rights tribunal; three to five years for a Charter challenge), can make legal remedies irrelevant to the lives of some disabled persons.

౿

CHAPTER 6

Dignity in Public Policy

The abuse of greatness is when it disjoins Remorse from power
William Shakespeare from *Julius Caesar,* Act II, Scene I

ONTARIO HAS TAKEN A LEAD ROLE in implementing policy that breaks down barriers for people with disabilities—first with the *Ontarians with Disabilities Act* (ODA), 2001 and now the *Accessibility for Ontarians with Disabilities Act* (AODA), a piece of remedial legislation that received Royal Assent on June 14, 2005.

There are some opportunities for optimism and for concern under the AODA, but as the founding Chair of the Ontario Accessibility Advisory Council, I was given a unique opportunity to view bureaucracy overtaking politics and political pretence being used to manipulate persons with disabilities while creating the impression that positive change was underway.

A series of policy initiatives have been introduced in recent years to address the needs of the disabled, in particular the Accessibility Advisory Council and Disability Directorate.

Creating a Disability Act

Since the passage of the *Americans with Disabilities Act* (ADA) in 1990, Canadians began discussing the possibility of a comprehensive piece of legislation for PWDs. This became particularly evident in the early 1990s when David Lepofsky and the Advocacy Resource Centre for the Handicapped (a legal clinic for PWDs) started to lobby the Ontario government to create an *Ontarians with Disabilities Act* (ODA). While the Ontario approach is quite different from that of the Americans, it appears that the ADA gave it inspiration.

The sincerity of the Ontario government was questioned from the start, particularly during the leadership of Ontario Premier Mike Harris, whose political ideology was right of centre, and whose government had single-handedly cut several social support programs fought for by persons with a disability and the poor during the previous 30 years. This skepticism was well-advised given that earlier drafts lacked enforcement mechanisms, and applied only to governmental services. A document that was to create progressive social policy could not be narrow and weak, or it would be doomed to failure.

I was somewhat more optimistic with the draft in the year 2000. I felt the government of Ontario should be congratulated for being the first jurisdiction in Canada to attempt to further remove the barriers faced by persons with a disability through the new ODA. It is extremely difficult to legislate the removal of prejudicial attitudes, but legislation can create a context for a more socially inclusive environment. These attitudes can be reshaped through greater working relationships and the development of mutually beneficial strategic plans.

The new ODA was to be a key step in achieving this goal of social integration of PWDs because it brought this community to the table in an equal and meaningful way. It is very important to note that ministries, government agencies, and municipalities would be held accountable for perpetuating barriers and would produce plans for their removal through an annual report. Considering the fact that these obstacles were a matter of much public awareness for over 30 years, it seemed that a bold new initiative was now necessary for their removal.

The bill was criticized for an apparent lack of enforcement options against wrongdoers. But there are strong enforcement mechanisms under the Ontario Human Rights Code and the legal standard under the code that compels the respondent to provide accommodations up to the point of undue financial hardship. Bringing a complaint to the Human Rights Commission, however, is a slow and frustrating process and this service can and should be improved.

The new ODA provided for the creation of the Accessibility Directorate and Accessibility Advisory Council of Ontario. A strong and committed directorate could provide a brilliant opportunity for the development of progressive guidelines and policies. A panel of experts working diligently to receive and advise upon annual reports could be a great asset to the minister in creating the vision and the implementation process for a barrier-free Ontario. Although the task of finding persons with the knowledge, diplomacy skills, and disability perspective required to bring the credibility to drive the potential of this legislation might prove difficult.

Finally, there was no mechanism in the act for alternative disputes resolution and/or mediation. The absence of mediation could lead to an adversarial process, pitting the Access Advisory Committee against all those that come before it, and/or allow for an accusation- and shame-based media circus where a minister or municipality is publicly flogged in the media.

Complaints under the ADA are usually resolved through mediation without the need of a hearing. Also, more than 80 percent of the cases brought to the Ontario Human Rights Board are successfully resolved through mediation. From this process, both the complainant and the respondent leave with a deal they can live with, their dignity intact, and with greater knowledge respecting how to function in a discrimination-free Ontario.

In effect, I was optimistic that the proposed *Ontarians with Disabilities Act* would be broad based, effective, and a key component in efforts to achieve equality at the Six Degrees of Dignity.

The Ontarians with Disabilities Act 2001

In December 2001, Ontario became the first Canadian jurisdiction to pass a disability act into law. The sections of the *Ontarians with Disabilities Act* (ODA) that were passed created the Accessibility Advisory Council of Ontario and the Disability Directorate of Ontario with all other sections expected to be proclaimed in the months shortly thereafter. Section 1 of the act outlines its purpose:

> To improve opportunities for persons with disabilities and to provide for their involvement in the identification, removal, and prevention of barriers to their full participation in the life of the province.

Further, the term "barrier" went far beyond the traditional notion of physical access by being defined as:

> …anything that prevents a person with a disability from fully participating

in all aspects of society because of his or her disability, including a physical barrier, an architectural barrier, an information or communications barrier, an attitudinal barrier, a technological barrier, a policy, or a practice.

To achieve its stated objectives, the ODA provided a framework for co-operation and conciliation that contrasted with the ADA. The ODA required the government to meet accessibility requirements in key areas of its activities and, among other things, to prepare accessibility plans. The legislation was expected to have an impact on services to the public, workplace policies and practices, buildings, publications, government Internet sites, purchasing procedures, and capital programs. The key to its success as it relates to enforcement and adherence to the act would be in greater public awareness, partnerships, excellence in report writing, continued resourcing, and ongoing enforcement through the complaint procedures of the Ontario Human Rights Code.

In addition to requiring several sectors to prepare accessibility plans, the ODA created bodies to promote the purposes of the act and to review the efficacy of its implementation. The principle players in these efforts were the Accessibility Advisory Council of Ontario, the Disability Directorate of Ontario, and local accessibility advisory committees that were to report to council in municipalities with more than 10,000 residents.

Accessibility Advisory Council of Ontario

To guide and assist the concerned sectors, the ODA created the Accessibility Advisory Council of Ontario, which was to report directly to the Minister of Citizenship.

The council was to bring together individuals who had the expertise, experience, and knowledge to provide strategic advice to the minister. It was to oversee implementation of the legislation. It was also charged with the responsibilities of monitoring and advancing the legislation, and providing annual reports on its activities. The council was to include persons with disabilities.

The terms of reference read that at the direction of the Minister of Citizenship, the council shall advise the minister on:
- the implementation of this act and the preparation of the regulations;
- the programs of public information related to this act;

- the accessibility for persons with disabilities to services provided or funded by the Government of Ontario;
- the accessibility for persons with disabilities to employment opportunities in economic sectors in Ontario; and
- all other matters related to the subject matter of this act that the minister directs.

The broad mandate of the Accessibility Advisory Council appeared to break new ground in the province of Ontario respecting an enforcement mechanism for the implementation of human rights legislation. The ODA rejected a litigation model and deferred administrative complaint procedures to the mechanisms under the Ontario Human Rights Code. Perhaps it may best be analogized to creatures of human rights legislation typically found within the purview of the United Nations. It was part tribunal, part mediator, part rapporteur, part commission, and part politician. Its evolution should have been one of great interest for commentators.

Accessibility Directorate of Ontario

The bureaucratic arm in the implementation of the act arose when, during the consultation process, participants expressed concerns about a lack of service delivery, attitudinal barriers, and the need for a single point of access to government where persons with disabilities could raise their concerns. For this, the Accessibility Directorate of Ontario was created. The Directorate was to address those concerns among others, and work with and across all of the sectors and ministries that are charged with responsibility for helping the government achieve its vision. It would also work with municipalities and the private sector to set standards and incentives for the removal of barriers on a sector-by-sector basis.

The Directorate was to launch a public education program to change attitudes and awareness. The campaign would deliver the message that "opening doors is everybody's business."

Prior to the ODA receiving Royal Assent, the dynamic and consumer-minded Minister of Citizenship, Cam Jackson, asked me to be the founding Chairperson of the Accessibility Advisory Council. This was truly a great honour, and a wonderful opportunity to develop progressive social policy for PWDs. I therefore immediately began discussions with the minister.

In the months before the contract was signed, the minister and his senior staff provided prospective members with their thoughts on the role of the council, its level of authority and its goals. Although each prospective member was spoken to on an individual basis, their impressions were consistent—that the council was to serve the minister while still remaining a semi-autonomous body. In that latter capacity it would oversee the ODA implementation process and provide advice to the minister regarding the act and its related activities. Council members were to be "disability ombudspersons" or "disability auditors." In addition, they expected to figure prominently in the development of accessibility plans; in the establishment of local accessibility councils; in the preparation of reports respecting the state of disability affairs of Ontario; and in the formulation of regulations aimed at a more inclusive Ontario. In effect, prospective members were led to believe that the council was to work in concert with the minister to advance and promote an agenda on behalf of Ontarians with disabilities—the principal goal being the prevention and removal of barriers, however constructed or deeply entrenched.

In addition to the above roles and responsibilities of the council, there was an indication that the chair would be expected to commit full-time, the vice-chair half-time, and all other members part-time. Likewise, to further these roles and responsibilities and to exemplify the esteem and authority appropriate to this newly formed council, the chair was expected to be given an authority analogous to the Executive Director of the Ontario Human Rights Commission and/or other senior positions.

All appeared to be in order for one of the best opportunities for PWDs in Ontario in a generation. Then Cam Jackson moved to a new portfolio, and was replaced by rookie Cabinet Minister Carl DaFaria. On reviewing the proposed first budget, and as a result of conversations with senior bureaucrats, it became clear that the bureaucracy had a significantly different impression of the roles and responsibilities of the council than I did.

To say the least, things from that point did not go well. Concerns respecting the inconsistency between the views of the bureaucrats and the council members were further outlined in a letter from me to senior bureaucrats. The contrasting views discussed were not resolved and it was determined that the best course of action would be an appeal to the minister.

I provided a written memo to the new minister where I advised that in order for the council to achieve a barrier-free Ontario it needed to be free to mobilize its diverse skills. Central to achieving this would be the erection and maintenance of a realistic operational framework. The success of such a framework depended on the council's budget and the nature of its relationship to the minister and the newly formed directorate.

At that early juncture, the relationships had not been clearly delineated. As a result, points of friction were emerging that were well-documented internally. In an effort to forestall difficulties, I attempted in that memo to outline the council's perception of its role and its relationship with the minister and the directorate. With these considerations in mind, I further recommended that a review of the council's proposed budget and its various relationships was warranted. In order that the council could begin its challenge on a firm footing, it was submitted that this review occur forthwith.

Because relationships were strained, a total of 17 recommendations were provided that would make the legislated responsibilities of the advisory council and the directorate operational. The review would also prevent a looming power struggle where ultimately PWDs would be the losers.

The minister was further advised that it would be a tragedy if, due to an inappropriate budget and blurred lines of authority, the role of the council were seen by the disability community as being weak and merely a figurehead. The excellent reception that this legislation first received may then very well be replaced by scorn.

The minister did not respond, and this was to have a prophetic ring to it because the incoming Liberal government was to scrap the legislation due to its ineffectiveness. By that time I had long since resigned because, as I had warned, the council became a figurehead with no authority to make decisions, public statements, be involved in policy and regulation development, or even make its own report public.

The AODA: A New Beginning

The ODA committee, led by David Lepofsky, continued to provide leadership in pushing the Ontario government to develop better legislation. They appear to have moved closer to success with the AODA (*Accessibility for Ontarians with Disabilities Act*). It establishes a process for developing and enforcing accessibility standards that will require organizations to remove barriers experienced by persons with disabilities. The AODA also contemplates local concerns by maintaining the municipal accessibility advisory committees established under the ODA. However, given the experience of the past as outlined previously, a healthy dose of caution or even cynicism may be advisable.

According to the AODA, the Minister of Citizenship and Immigration will create standard development committees, each responsible for a specific industry or sector. Invited to participate on these committees will be persons with disabilities (or their representatives), industry representatives, and the ministries responsible for those industries. The committees will determine long-term accessibility objectives for the specified sector and time frames (maximum of five years) for their progressive implementation. The proposed standards are to name or describe the persons or organizations they cover. The committees will develop a proposed accessibility standard and provide it to the minister. The minister will then make the standard available for public comment for 45 days by posting it on a government website. After considering the comments received, the committee may amend the standard accordingly and provide the new proposed standard to the minister. Within five years of a standard being adopted into regulation, the committee will review the objective and time frames previously developed and propose another standard.

The minister, advised by the Accessibility Directorate and after consulting with other ministries, may enact the standards through regulation. The minister may exempt certain persons or organizations from the application of the standards and may enter into incentive agreements encouraging organizations to surpass the requirements of the standards.

Each organization that is subject to a standard is required to file an annual accessibility report with the director (who is appointed by the minister) and make it available to the public. If an organization fails to comply with reporting or any other requirement, the director may order the organization to pay an administrative penalty.

The minister may appoint inspectors to ensure compliance with the standards. These inspectors are able to enter private property to monitor compliance.

They are also able to obtain search warrants and the assistance of the police, if necessary.

The minister can designate one or more tribunals that will be responsible for hearing matters arising under the act as specified in their designation. The tribunal(s) may hear appeals of an organization subject to an order because of non-compliance with an incentive agreement, reporting requirements, payment of administrative penalties, compliance with standards, and so on.

If an organization fails to comply with an order of the tribunals or the directors, and there is no appeal, the order may be filed with the Superior Court of Justice and enforced as an order of that court. The act also specifies that certain actions or omissions can be the subject of provincial offences.

The powers under the AODA are far more expansive than the ODA. It applies to all sectors of the economy, including the private sector. It provides for the development of a comprehensive set of accessibility standards to remove barriers and achieve full inclusion. As well, it provides for the participation of persons with disabilities throughout the process. However, the legislation is vague on how they are included, and who is considered an appropriate PWD. There also is no direct complaint mechanism for a PWD.

These enforcement mechanisms may potentially be weakened should the directorate allow itself to be overly politicized. Also, there remains the question of whether the advisory council will be of any utility at all due to the fact that it is not even quasi-independent, and there is no guarantee that it will have direct access to the minister.

In addition, the act, by creating numerous tribunals with the power to make orders, potentially creates a host of problems. This seems bizarre when the usual approach is to create one tribunal that would hear appeals under the AODA. This allows expertise to develop within the tribunal, and encourages a consistency of decision making through the cohesiveness of one body. In addition, a single tribunal can more successfully achieve a key purpose of administrative bodies, which is to bridge the divide between law and policy, and through this create a sound, effective, and independently developed policy that can best benefit persons with disabilities.

There is also concern about Section 27 (3) regarding "a resistance to oral submissions." This is legislation that is remedial in nature, and is creating public policy. It appears less than assistive to cloister the decision making of these tribunals through a narrowing of the process to the receipt of only written submissions.

Still the newly formed Accessibility Standards Advisory Council (ASAC) acts exclusively at the direction of the minister. If recent history is any indication, then it is best to read into that, that the advisory council will be fully controlled by the bureaucracy while ignored or held at arms length by the politicians.

Human Rights Complaints in Ontario

In Ontario, it is illegal for anyone to discriminate against another person on the basis of age, gender, ethnic origin, religion, or sexuality, and everyone has the right to be treated fairly in all areas of society, including the workplace, the home, schools, and the courts. The law protects the inherent dignity and worth of every person and provides for equal rights and opportunities without discrimination in the following areas:

- accommodation or housing;
- contracts or formal agreements;
- employment (how employers advertise, interview, hire, treat, and promote employees);
- goods and facilities (e.g., hospitals and schools);
- membership in trade unions;
- services (e.g., restaurants, stores, theatres);
- vocational or occupational associations.

Any individual who believes she or he has been discriminated against in one of the above areas can file a complaint with the Ontario Human Rights Commission. The commission has an established process for registering complaints, procedures for mediation, investigation, conciliation, case analysis, decision making, and/or for referring the matter for a hearing before the independent quasi-judicial administrative body, the Ontario Human Rights Tribunal.

I am a former part-time member of the Human Rights Tribunal. The intellectual vigour and sensitivity that all members brought to their decision making made this one of the most satisfying and exciting work experiences of my career. Under the leadership of Chair Matthew Garfield, the tribunal took excellence in legal understanding, and advancement of human rights norms one step further by fostering a strong programme of mediation and alternative dispute resolution. Filing a human rights complaint, should a person with a disability feel that he or she has been discriminated against, remains a critically important option in the advancement of disability rights. The AODA appears to offer some initiative in the long-term objective to achieve a barrier-free Ontario, but its focus, independence from political meddling, and enforcement mechanisms means that it will have to go far in order to gain credibility. The Ontario Human Rights Code offers one step further in broadening the protection of human rights in Ontario and beyond.[20]

~

---

20. For more information about the complaints process visit the OHRC website:
http://www.ohrc.on.ca /english/complaints/index.shtml

CHAPTER 7

Dignity of Self

The Puck Dances Lovingly

" I'm alone, except for equipment, stick, and puck as I skate, grinding the ice with each pivot and turn. The puck dances, flipping off the end of my stick, slipping between my feet until it is caught by the blade of a skate and kicked forward, perfectly, to the awaiting stick. And, again in unison, the partnership of man, stick, and puck dances lovingly across the green ice.

Yes, green ice. The ice is always a faint lime or ocean green with faded blue and red lines. Fog is usually lifting off of the opposite end. There is no one in the surrounding semi-lit bleachers, although you sense from the hollow echoes, there must be someone nearby, if for no other reason than to drive the Zamboni and keep the rink secure.

The motion of me, the player, then returns. This is no longer just butterfly-like movement of puck and player. It has risen in intensity. I begin skating in very quick bursts, feeling the tug of exertion deep in my gut as each muscle cries for blood and each vein for oxygen. Sometimes I'll shoot the puck into an empty net, or slap it against the board, hanging my thoughts on the resonating smack throughout the arena.

This speed is absolute delight—freedom unending except for those fucking four-foot white boards. Bold, flat, faceless, like a sheer cliff dropping into winter's frozen Lake Superior. They stop me. Create discord between the marriage of puck and player—I'm penned in. And, as I let these bursts of speed fly me across the ice, I become angered by the boards, beginning to realize I'm only going in circles with a toy-like puck. It gives delight, but is loyal only to the ice.

I then square off before the boards in an attempt to overcome these imposed limitations, skating back and forth across the blue lines or end to end as fast as possible—still holding puck against stick. But, this effort is as vain as a gored and exhausted bull making full charge against a matador, and the matador awaiting, sword pointed forward, nerves piqued and eyes fixed on the bull's spinal cord—knowing this will be the bull's last run.

Finally, I stop. Pleasure has stopped. I rest on one knee. Now with head bowed and uncomfortable sweat around my neck and eyes.

The image complete, my thoughts shift. The ice is gone. My day continues. **"**

⌒

We have discussed barriers and challenges that can lead to discrimination against persons with disabilities. Through poetry and consideration of familial relationships, including parenting with a disability, this chapter will examine how to construct an authentic self that evolves beyond internalized subordination, to empowerment and the overcoming of alienation. At its core is self-esteem, and self-worth, and to achieve this end it is critical to explore one's creative abilities, to express the emotional and spiritual passion that they can produce, and to find most trusted relationships. Matters of body image, personal identity, and self-esteem are central to any discussion on the nature of dignity. As such, while it transcends all conceptual figuring of what is equality, a positive self-image is a critical component of the Six Degrees of Dignity that should be explored.

"Self-esteem, believed to be a major factor of our self-concept, may be considered as an individual's global positive or negative feelings toward himself or herself." A person's self-esteem also affects the manner in which he or she deals with the environment. That is, people with low self-esteem tend to view their environment as threatening, and, therefore, have difficulty interacting in it. People with high self-esteem, however, tend to deal more actively with their environment, are better able to meet environmental demands, and generally feel more secure about themselves."[21]

While working on this chapter, I called my friend Irmo Marini, who is a professor of Rehabilitation Psychology, and has worked extensively in the area of self-esteem and disability to further discuss his perspectives on achieving dignity and self-worth as a person with a disability. Dr. Marini also had a spinal injury about seven months prior to mine. He has always provided the support and inherent knowledge that both a peer and mentor can provide, and this seemed a great opportunity to again glean from his expertise. My point to him was that I believe the essence of self-worth is found through love, whether it be for community, family, or an individual. As John Lennon sang, "all you need is love." In Dr. Marini's unique way of providing positive manipulation, he partly agreed with this premise. He also noted that self-esteem can be found through achievements in other areas, including job satisfaction, social position, academic excellence, and athletic success.

Should those areas of positive stimuli be reinforced in early child development and later, then the individual will probably develop a strong internal locus of control. In other words, these individuals are self-confident, and with this have sophisticated coping abilities.

Vulnerabilities, however, occur when a person with a disability does not have a strong internal locus of control, and external stimuli such as an insult or condescending remark can be personally devastating. Within a broader context of discrimination where negative stereotyping is frequently reinforced upon individuals with a disability, they may find themselves not just living with physical, but also emotional paralysis. At that point, the world can be ramped with gold and the best human rights laws conceivable enforced, but if they do not have any self-esteem, there will be an internalized barrier that precludes them from meaningful participation with their family, community, and themselves as psycho-spiritual beings.

My discussion with Dr. Marini reminded me of many examples of individuals I meet as clients in my family law practice in the areas of access and custody or child welfare. At the point individuals need my services, they often have arrived at the end of a dysfunctional relationship and are now estranged from

---

21. Marini, I., Rogers, L., Slate, J.R., and Vines, C. (1995). "Self-esteem Differences Among Persons With Spinal Cord Injury," *Rehabilitation Counseling Bulletin*, 38(3), 198-206.

their partners. Frequently, they are in a state of very low self-esteem because the negative dynamics of their relationship have resulted in the systematic erosion of their self-confidence. They may have experienced physical, emotional, verbal, or financial abuse. This did not happen overnight in a cataclysmic crushing of the self, but was an insidious plucking of a former sense of self-worth that had been under a barrage of insults such as "you're stupid," "you never do anything for me," "you're fat," or "you have ruined our sex life." That individual is shocked by how far they have let things deteriorate and now must reclaim their own sense of dignity. If they fail to do so, the result is most often a failure to have a full life and to reconnect with friends and society.

Quite sadly, I have had clients so low that, against my advice, they have returned to an abusive relationship, although they knew that this would mean that the Children's Aid Society would apprehend their children and seek an order from the court that access be denied for the purposes of adoption with another family. I have also seen parents willing to deny themselves access to their children, although they love them deeply, because they have endured such persistent emotional and verbal abuse from their ex-partner that they are intimidated by the continued suffering of their self-esteem that they will have to endure. It has further been my experience that neither gender is immune to such a disability of the self.

Love and Family

With a broad spectrum of avenues toward a strong internal locus of control considered, this chapter must also reflect a lived perspective, or in other words, perspective of the self. It is best described as a subjective articulation rather than the objective overview of an expert. Indeed, it is not being written by a rehabilitation psychologist. With this in mind, the following considers a journey towards self-hood through love and family.

This poem touches upon the risk, pain, reward and growth of romantic love, and its critical necessity to developing the whole person, whether they are with or without a disability.

A Letter and Memory

I

I reached for the brown
sun-drenched skin that spoke to
me of summer. Looking into
my eyes, she placed her arm on
my shoulder, raising the
flowing floral pattern of her
dress. It now moved in the
peering light—the only thing
between us and the silent
twilight breeze from the ocean below.

II

DEAR M.

Things have ended with G. It has made
me sad. For some reason, a choke hold
was put on the relationship in January,
and it was left to suffocate from then
onward. I think her parents created the
impression, that if she were with me, she
would have to give up her family, culture,
and all she had known. G. doesn't
really want to take the world by storm.
She's fairly satisfied in her home town
(though not terribly happy). And, although
this perception created by her parents
is untrue, I don't think she wanted to
make the sacrifices she may have had
to in order to be with me.

And me. I'm searching to a degree, and
finding myself and my life. I think I had
hoped my life would develop in her direction
and we should grow together. Maybe
there were sacrifices on my part, that
I was unwilling to make (certainly, there
were).

Whatever is the truth between the possibilities,
I don't know. I do know I had fallen in
love with her and found something very
beautiful in what we shared. I miss her
very much.

Yours D.

III

This first tear has formed
without your blessing.

It asserts the rules to be.
Inside, holding full the chemistry
that made my blood yours—
on the first moment
of the first evening, you said
you never knew
these hands were meant to show you
love

The garden of that nightfall
sung; "This is the rose's home.
Welcome the summer's warmth
and let this night of the perfect moon
pull you to its softness."

This tear now shines
on the last hour of our last moon.

Rolling over the sandbar of my eyelash
Ignoring every barrier.
Like your eyes next to mine,
when your dark hair tumbled
and your lips held mine
the morning of our arms intertwined.

IV

Sight is now inside me
as sister tears join in
a cataract of hesitance
the next thought is nothing.

These tears of my framework existence
reach across the ocean
that is ours to share,
one by one they fall
answering the emptiness of my parted
mouth like a shoreline accepting the
salt sting of each ending wave.

They then wash away my last refuge;
manhood and words.
The heart that showed you too little
yet everything.
The art that held us fulfilled
yet incomplete.

V

On this, the last day of our hands stretch
across an ocean to know beauty
in the meeting of a fingertip,
Please allow our memory when you
take communion.

Remember my hand under yours
when we lifted our palms to the blue sky
wanting the grass to hold us downward,
and the sun to never let our spirit
touch the ground.

Remember my eyes to yours
when our arms moved forward
or hand to touch cheek or mouth
or body to touch tongue.

Remember this body,
that livened with arms raised
to meet each brief whisper
in the belief on earth was the time of
forever.

I included this poem because so much has been made about discrimination being a barrier to finding and/or losing love. It is also an important illustration of the fact that breaking the bonds of bigotry is not a one-way ticket to lotus land; it is more about removing paternalistic insulating barriers to equal participation. That means full realization of the human condition with its accomplishments, triumphs, loss, and wonderful discovery through love.

Parenting With a Disability

Because discrimination historically has been a barrier to parenting for PWDs, it is very important to this community to be aware of laws and perspectives that may be potential inhibitors to raising children. The United Nations has called the family the fundamental structure in the development of society. This may be a critical indicator of the international consensus surrounding the importance of family in achieving full social and cultural participation. If discrimination denies this to PWDs, then their desire to have a family by traditional or non-traditional means can be expected to escalate.

Until recently, it was impossible for many persons with spinal cord injury (SCI) and other disabilities to become parents. But, intra-cyto plasmic sperm injection, electro-ejaculation, and other forms of new reproductive technologies have brought exciting breakthroughs resulting in a wave of optimism amongst expectant and new parents with a disability. This new horizon of opportunities raises the question, what are their legal rights?

On some occasions, child welfare workers, social workers, and rehabilitation team members have shown a bias against persons with a disability becoming parents because of a presumption that persons with a mobility impairment do not have the physical capacity for proper child nurturing. Can these agencies and professionals be barriers to prospective parents? Do they have a role in supporting child development? How can parents with a disability assert their rights to custody without concern that this will receive a dim view from child welfare agencies and/or the courts? And does a parent with a disability have legal rights equal to an able-bodied person?

A physical disability may create a perception that there are limitations in meeting some parenting duties, especially with babies and toddlers; however, PWDs are most often experts in assessing barriers and finding opportunities to overcome obstacles. The strong skill set of many persons with a disability to develop support networks for personal care needs to be emphasized and recognized by society and the courts because, logically, these support networks could extend to parenting.

It is these contradictions that will confront a judge when applying the "best interest of the child" doctrine. They also establish an excellent framework for PWDs to consider when changing attitudes about their ability to parent. They are:

- The love, affection and emotional ties between the child and each person claiming custody and/or access, and/or persons involved in the care and upbringing of the child;
- The views and preference of the child. This generally translates into the opinion of children between the ages of 10 and 14 being highly influential, and those over 14 wholly determinative;
- The length of time the child has lived in a stable home environment. Usually a court will not order that the child leave its home if it is in a secure environment;
- The ability and willingness of each person applying for custody to provide the child with guidance and education, necessary for life and any

special needs;

- The permanence and stability of the family unit with which it is proposed the child will live;
- The relationship by blood or through an adoption order of the child, and each reason to do otherwise.

It behoves the parent with a disability to apply their considerable skills and capabilities in developing personal care plans and child care plans. Also, there is an important role for agencies to play in providing personal care assistance to both parent and child when necessary. In general, social service agencies should consider the unique skills and love that parents with a disability can bring to child development.

With this, persons with a disability can look forward to parenting with confidence that their coping, planning skills, and capabilities acquired out of necessity will serve them well should questions of custody and access need to be judicially considered.

Again, love through parenting can bring pain that the law does not describe:

> The photo of that pony ride
> is now taped to my fridge
> a token to the almost happiness we have.
> your small blond hair
> and inexplicable smile
> full of goodbye.
>
> The wind caught you cold
> against the brick of your daycare's wall
> that day
> But when the sun touched
> your shoulders in the playground
> you no longer clung to my chest for
> warmth
> you announced "this is my daddy,
> come meet my daddy."

Then your hat was painted and
sprinkled with sparkles
a shiny love promise
that you would later wear while
holding the stuffed polar bear that you
call doggy (it fading and threadbare at
the neck from the countless comfort that
it has brought you in your young sleeps).

I didn't like that photo
when it first arrived—
your head small and puny
in a world where every day
you made magnificent choices

Now adult choices
and adult wrongs
are your wrongs—
sparkle fragments are retrieved by the
telephone and weekend visits
where you disappear beside hello.

∽

CHAPTER 8

Dignity in Future

Here vigour fail'd the towering fantasy:
But yet the will roll'd onward, like a wheel
In even motion, by a love impelled,
That moves the sun in heaven and all the stars

Dante from *Paradise—Canto XXXIII*

SEVERAL ISOLATED EFFORTS at a domestic level in Canada have brought mixed results in efforts to reduce discrimination, but an international example that offers much hope for the future is the UN Convention on the Rights and Dignity of Persons with a Disability (UNCRDPWD) currently being negotiated by all member states. On August 25, 2006, all UN member states adopted the Convention during meetings in New York. At the time of this writing, the draft Convention is being prepared for submission to the UN General Assembly for ratification in the fall of 2006.

This international human rights treaty combines the protection of individual and group rights while creating a framework for positive policy and public perception changes. Furthermore, the efficacy of the Convention will be monitored through a system of report writing, and greater enforcement will be assured through negotiation of an Optional Protocol, which creates a quasi-judicial body that can receive individual complaints for a breach of any Article of the Convention. Should the UN choose to support this convention with a properly financed administrative structure, there may be created one more cog in the wheel toward the Six Degrees of Dignity.

The International Context: Dignity Denied

As a group, PWDs compose some 600 million people worldwide, of whom approximately 80 percent live in developing countries. People with disabilities are a sizable constituency. More dramatic than mere statistics, however, is the appalling human rights condition of people with disabilities in both the developed and the developing world.

Persons with disabilities across the globe are routinely subjected to discrimination in a wide range of social contexts, including the workplace, schools, health care facilities, government, and recreational facilities. Lack of access to such basic needs as housing, education, health care, employment, and mobility in the environment has resulted in extreme poverty, social exclusion, and poor health. Exclusion and unequal access to resources are only part of the picture. PWDs often face human rights abuses, including involuntary institutionalization, incarceration, forced abortion, sterilization, and psychiatric drugging. As a socially and economically disempowered group, PWDs have little or no influence in public policy process and have consistently been excluded from participating in decisions that affect their daily survival. While some governments and societies have adopted a social inclusion and rights-based approach to disability issues, many still rely on an outdated charity model or a narrow medical model that spotlights medical "solutions" without addressing the socio-economic reality of disability. National or international legal mechanisms designed to protect and promote the rights of PWDs are nonexistent or inadequate and reinforce stereotypical perceptions of PWDs. Disability has traditionally not been prioritized on the agendas of international human rights institutions, and the mainstream movement has yet to mark disability as a core human rights concern.

Throughout the world, people with disabilities are subject to de jure and de facto discrimination: they are denied jobs, excluded from schools, are considered unworthy of marriage or partnership, and are even barred from certain religious practices. The underlying attitude that disabled persons have intrinsically less value because of their disabilities has devastating implications for disabled persons around the world. As noted earlier, social psychologists have described the way in which oppressed groups who have been systematically denied power and influence in the society in which they live, internalize negative messages about their abilities, and so often come to accept them as their "truth." Members of the disability community have documented compelling personal accounts of disability oppression. Internalized oppression works in combination with economic and social contexts and serves to restrict options that people perceive as open to them and legitimate for them. Empowerment rests in tackling the negative assumptions that society and disabled people themselves have made about what they can and cannot do.

As the first UN Special Rapporteur on Disability, Leandro Despouy observed in 1991 that persons with disabilities:

> frequently live in deplorable conditions, owing to the presence of physical and social barriers, which prevent their integration and full participation in the community. As a result, millions of children and adults throughout the world are segregated and deprived of virtually all their rights and lead a wretched, marginal life.

Adequate health care, housing, education, and meaningful employment are of fundamental importance to all human beings, including disabled people. Yet millions of disabled people around the world do not have access to the resources necessary to fulfill these basic needs, nor do they have influence over the policy decisions that affect their daily struggle for survival.

A Special Convention on Disability

Ironically, while the rights of individuals with disabilities are protected within a broad human rights framework based on the Universal Declaration of Human Rights and the International Bill of Human Rights, no explicit mention is made of discrimination on the grounds of disability. Growing awareness of this deficiency has led to the realization that the rights of PWDs should be the subject of a specialized convention elaborating the full range of human rights.

It has inspired what Quinn and Degener have termed the "twin track approach." Essentially it calls first for exploitation of existing human rights norms and legislation through advocacy before existing judicial, quasi-judicial, and monitoring bodies, for example, the UN Committee on Civil and Political Rights. Secondly, it promotes the advancement of disability rights through a comprehensive treaty that articulates the full range of rights aimed at removing disability-based discrimination, and in addition contains mechanisms to enforce these rights.[22]

From Voluntary to Enforceable Measures

While the UN had been founded upon a belief in the inherent dignity of all members of the human family, persons with a disability were clearly a community of concern yet one that did not receive the same attention as those who were discriminated against based on race, ethnicity, sex, religion, age, or were subject to torture or cruel and inhumane treatment. As an international body arising from the ashes of World War II, and the Nuremburg War Crimes Tribunal where some of the worst Nazi perpetrators of the genocide against European Jews were tried, this is not entirely surprising. We should not forget, however, that Gypsies, homosexuals, communists, political prisoners, priests, and the disabled were also exterminated by the Nazis on a mass scale. Still, historic pressures in the 20th century were causing civil rights movements, such as the African American protests in the United States and the rise of feminism, to gain international focus for redress of profound and systemic discrimination based on race and gender.

The genesis of disability-based rights promotion is generally considered to be 1981, which was declared the UN Year of the Disabled Person. It was followed by the World Programme of Action Concerning Disabled Persons, adopted by the UN General Assembly at its 37th regular session on December 3, 1982. It sought an "analysis of the situation of disabled persons…within the context of different levels of economic and social development and different cultures." Although creating voluntary targets, it recognized that the international community could be an effective force in preventing causes of disability, including disease, malnutrition, environmental pollution, poor hygiene, and inadequate health care, and specifically emphasizes that the ultimate responsibility for addressing the conditions and consequences of disability rests with governments.

The inception of the World Programme of Action continues to have a profound impact on raising awareness and promoting disability rights. December 3rd is now celebrated throughout the world as the international day of the

22. *Human Rights and Disability: The current use and future potential of United Nations human rights instruments in the context of disability.* Gerard Quinn and Theresia Degener, ©United Nations 2002, Office of the High Commissioner for Human Rights.

disabled person. It is an opportunity for many governmental bodies and disability NGOs to plan special events that recognize the dignity and inherent self-worth of PWDs. So far, I am unaware of a pride parade, but that may be yet to come…and the reader can draw conjecture as to what would be the winning costumes and parade floats, or whether there would be any body piercings.

Beyond voluntary measures and special events, efforts by states such as Mexico and Ireland have maintained the momentum for treaty development. General Assembly resolution 56/168 of December 19, 2001, initiated by Mexico, established an ad hoc committee "to consider proposals for a comprehensive and integral international convention to promote and protect the rights and dignity of persons with disabilities, based on the holistic approach in the work done in the fields of social development, human rights, and non-discrimination."

The first session of the committee, which took place from July 29 to August 9, 2002, highlighted "a shift in focus from care, social welfare, and medical support to an emphasis on the human rights framework necessary to pursue the goals of full participation of persons with disabilities in economic, social, and political life, and development on the basis of equality." At that meeting, the committee recommended that deliberations would continue at a second session to be held in May/June 2003. The primary goal going into the 2003 session was to affirm the need for a new convention within the UN system. Issues before the committee were to include: "the scope and purpose of the proposed convention, the areas it should cover, and its relation to existing conventions and instruments, including the Standard Rules on the Equalization of Opportunities for Persons with Disabilities, adopted by the General Assembly in 1993." In addition, this process of treaty drafting has been unique by ensuring that PWDs themselves should play a leadership role in mainstreaming disability within existing human rights instruments, and in developing the UNCRDPWD.

At the meeting of January 5 to 16, 2004, there was general agreement on the chair's suggestion to discuss the following aspects of the convention:

1. Preamble;
2. Objectives and General Principles;
3. Scope and Definitions;
4. Guarantee of Equality and Non-Discrimination;
5. Guarantee of Specific Rights;

6. National Implementation Mechanism.

By the end of the discussions, these areas had been developed and articles had been drafted.

Benefits of a Disability Convention

In a submission before the Parliamentary Subcommittee for Persons with Disabilities, Steve Estey, Chair of the Council of Canadians with Disabilities International Committee, and I argued for Canadian support for this UN convention at a time when it was receiving much resistance in government circles. As we indicated, the current effort to secure the adoption of an international convention on the rights of people with disabilities has much to offer. The most significant advantages include:

1. Providing an immediate statement of international legal accountability regarding disability rights;

2. Clarifying the content of human rights principles and their application to people with disabilities;

3. Providing an authoritative and global reference point for domestic law and policy initiatives;

4. Providing mechanisms for more effective monitoring, including reporting on the enforcement of the convention by governments and non-governmental organizations, supervision by a body of experts mandated by the convention, and possibly the consideration of individual or group complaints under a mechanism to be created by the convention;

5. Establishing a useful framework for international cooperation;

6. Providing a fair and common standard of assessment and achievement across cultures and levels of economic development; and

7. Creating a broad forward-looking rights-based consensus providing transformative educative benefits for all participants engaged in the preparatory and formal negotiation phases, and for the public as countries consider ratification of the convention.

Fortunately, some years down the road, I am pleased to say that the Canadian government is now playing an active and positive role in the ongoing negotiations to draft, pass, and ratify this convention.

What Is a Treaty and How Should It Be Structured?

A treaty is defined in the Vienna Convention on The Law of Treaties as, "an international agreement concluded between states in written form and governed by international law, whether embodied in a single instrument or in two or more related instruments and whatever its particular designation." It therefore creates a framework for conduct between countries, and expectations within the world communities on how it will treat its citizens. It is within these terms that principles are articulated and enforcement mechanisms are created to bring evolution of norms through debate, advocacy, reporting, and/or decision making.

Treaty drafting should begin with a clear sense of purpose—why it should exist and what it will achieve.

When the purpose and principles have been established, the contents follow a fairly consistent structure. While it is not written in stone, a treaty generally includes the following:

- Introductory paragraphs (usually preamble that outlines principles and purpose, and definitions);
- Substantive obligations;
- Implementation techniques and monitoring provisions.

Why Make a Treaty?

It can be argued that the protection of human rights and, with this, disability rights, programs, and policy are now normative in countries throughout the world. Furthermore, existing legal regimes and mechanisms provide a forum for continued advancements. Amongst those are domestic human rights codes, constitutions, and such international legislations as the Universal Declaration on Human Rights, the International Covenant on Civil and Political Rights (ICCPR) and the International Covenant on Economic Social and Cultural Rights. These legal and policy regimes, however, beg three questions:

1. Do they promote non-discrimination and dignity for PWDs in a meaningful way at the domestic level?

2. Can countries share their findings and perspectives in the advancement of disability rights?

3. Are PWDs able to exploit these legal and policy regimes in order to advocate for disability rights?

If these questions are not answered in the affirmative, nations will often look to treaties and treaty making to resolve apparent gaps.

Implementation and Treaty Influence in Canada

Internal Ratification Process

In Canada, treaty making is an Executive act, derived from the Royal Prerogative, meaning Parliamentary approval is not required for Canada to enter into international treaties. Although only the federal executive is empowered to enter into international treaties, the federal government cannot legislate to implement treaties in areas that would otherwise fall within provincial jurisdiction. As human rights matters are a shared federal–provincial jurisdiction, the general practice is to ratify only a human rights treaty after obtaining the support of Canadian provinces and territories.

Typically, as a prelude to ratification, Department of Justice officials consult with colleagues in other affected federal departments and agencies, as well as with the provinces, territories, Aboriginal groups and other non-governmental groups, to determine:

- Whether existing domestic laws and policies already conform to the treaty obligations;
- If there are inconsistencies, whether new legislation/policies should be adopted or whether existing legislation/policies should be amended;
- Alternatively, whether it is appropriate to maintain the domestic position even though it is inconsistent with a treaty provision, and enter a reservation.

Reservations are employed where the domestic position appears to be inconsistent and cannot be changed for various reasons. Statements of understanding may also be used to assert how Canada views the interpretation of the treaty provisions to ensure that domestic legislation is consistent. Where there is uncertainty as to whether a domestic measure is consistent with a treaty obligation, a legal opinion may be sought.

Dualist System

Canada follows what is termed a "dualist approach" to making international treaties law domestically. This means that in order for the treaty obligations to be given the force of law domestically, they must first be passed through the appropriate provincial and/or federal legislative process. As a further result, international treaties in Canada cannot by themselves create a cause of action, and Canadian courts cannot give any order pursuant to the treaty. This is similar in approach to other countries such as the United States, United Kingdom, Australia, and New Zealand.

It should also be noted that with respect to customary international law, Canada's approach is "monist" (where international obligations automatically become domestic laws, in contradistinction to the dualist system) in the sense that customary international law automatically forms part of our domestic law. However, domestic legislation would prevail in the event of any inconsistency.

As a general rule, human rights treaties are not incorporated into domestic legislation. This is often due to the fact that the same obligation appears in other international and domestic human rights instruments. For example, the ICCPR contains a guarantee of freedom of expression. The government fears that to legislate different freedom of expression guarantees—which are worded in different ways—could result in inconsistent legislative statements, and it is, at a minimum, a confusing legislative policy approach.

Influence on the Courts

Canada's dualist system may limit the court's ability to directly employ international treaties; however, treaty obligations have a strong influence on the interpretation of domestic legislation.

With respect to ordinary legislation, the courts have said that judges should strive to interpret such laws in accordance with relevant international obligations. In a recent decision of the Supreme Court of Canada, the court stated that the "values reflected in international human rights law may help inform the contextual approach to statutory interpretation and judicial review." However, if the express provisions of a domestic statute are contrary to or inconsistent with Canada's international obligations, the former prevails.

It appears constitutional provisions are to also be influenced by international treaty obligations. As former Chief Justice Dickson said:

"Though I do not believe the judiciary is bound by the norms of international law in interpreting the Charter, their norms provide a relevant and persuasive source for interpreting of the provisions of the Charter, especially when they arise out of Canada's international obligation under rights conventions."[23]

Therefore, although the judiciary is not bound to apply Canada's international human rights treaty obligations, they will attempt to bring any discussions in conformity with their terms.

Mobilizing Public Opinion

In addition to influencing legislative change during the ratification process and subsequent judicial decision making, international human rights treaties can have a powerful effect on public opinion. Human rights monitoring mechanisms create a highly credible level of appeal when domestic remedies have been exhausted. Essentially, a finding of a treaty breach by an international human rights monitoring body, for example, tribunal, rapporteur, or committee would be a criticism against Canada by the world community. Generally, the Canadian government and the Canadian public are loath to be embarrassed in such a fashion. As a result, NGOs and First Nations have been able to use the UN Human Rights Committee and the UN Committee on Economic Social and Cultural Rights to gain public support and bring legislative change in Canada.

We are left to wonder if, within the complexities of Canada's federal and bureaucratic structure, ratification will be easy. It is expected that the UNCRDPWD will be open for signature in the late fall or early winter of 2006. The legal drafters are currently reviewing the text in its draft form to confirm that there are no technical errors in the writing. It has been through the very end stages of what is termed "a legal scrub," and it will be ready for the United Nations General Assembly. The ratification process may prove to be another barrier that disability NGOs through lobbying and public pressure may have to overcome.

---

23. *Reference Re Public Service Employee Relations Act (Alta)*, pages 349-50. See also *Baker v. Canada (Minister of Citizenship and Immigration), (1999) 2 S.C.R. 817.*

Canada's International Commitment to Disability Rights

Since the adoption of the Universal Declaration of Human Rights by the United Nations in 1948, Canada has made a plethora of commitments to persons with a disability under the microscope of the world community. Central among these have been the Covenant on Civil and Political Rights, and the Covenant on Economic, Social and Cultural Rights, the interpretation of which is discussed further below. The Committee on Economic, Social and Cultural Rights noted this broad commitment to persons with a disability and noted additional international instruments of relevance:

> The international community has affirmed its commitment to ensuring the full range of human rights for persons with disabilities in the following instruments: (a) the World Programme of Action concerning Disabled Persons, which provides a policy framework aimed at promoting "effective measures for prevention of *disability*, rehabilitation and the realization of the goals of "full participation" of [persons with disabilities] in social life and development, and of "equality"; (b) the Guidelines for the Establishment and Development of National Coordinating Committees on *Disability* or Similar Bodies, adopted in 1990; (c) the Principles for the Protection of Persons with Mental Illness and for the Improvement of Mental Health Care, adopted in 1991; (d) the Standard Rules on the Equalization of Opportunities for Persons with Disabilities (hereinafter referred to as the "Standard Rules"), adopted in 1993, the purpose of which is to ensure that all persons with disabilities "may exercise the same rights and obligations as others." *The Standard Rules are of major importance and constitute a particularly valuable reference guide in identifying more precisely the relevant obligations of States parties under the Covenant."* [Emphasis added.]

As Rule 5 of the UN Standard Rules on the Equalization of Opportunities for Persons with Disabilities states:

> States should recognize the overall importance of accessibility in the process of the equalization of opportunities in all spheres of society. For persons with disabilities of any kind, States should (a) introduce programmes of

action to make the physical environment accessible; and (b) undertake measures to provide access to information and communication.

(a) Access to the physical environment
1. States should initiate measures to remove the obstacles to participation in the physical environment. Such measures should be to develop standards and guidelines and to consider enacting legislation to *ensure accessibility to various areas in society*, such as housing, buildings, *public transport services* and other means of transportation, streets and other outdoor environments. […]" [Emphasis added.]

The World Program of Action Concerning Disabled Persons recognized that the international community could be an effective force in preventing causes of disability, including disease, malnutrition, environmental pollution, poor hygiene and inadequate health care, and specifically emphasizes that the ultimate responsibility for addressing the conditions and consequences of disability rests with governments.

More recently, Canada's commitment to persons with a disability has been evident in its wholehearted participation in the UNCRDPWD drafting process. As noted earlier, many member states and numerous NGO participants should be congratulated for having seen the draft convention adopted in August 2006. It will be before the UN General Assembly in the fall of 2006, and it is hoped that it will be passed and the work of so many can be celebrated. This new thematic international human rights treaty will elaborate existing human rights norms within a disability context, while creating a framework for positive policy and public perception changes, consistent with the World Program of Action's emphasis on government responsibility for addressing the conditions and consequences of disability.

The Twin Track Approach: Domestic and International Law

The twin track approach, which includes promoting ratification of the convention and advocating for disability rights before domestic courts, was recently played out before the Supreme Court of Canada in the matter of *Council of*

Canadians with Disabilities v. VIA Rail. The decision, which is pending, may be an indicator of the efficacy of the twin track approach as it relates to international human rights norms, and whether disability NGOs should consider it as a viable strategic option.

During a submission to the United Nations Committee on Economic, Social and Cultural Rights, the Government of Canada indicated that it agreed with the position that international human rights law should comport with domestic law to the greatest degree possible because it plays a critical role in the evolution of its legal norms:

> International human rights conventions that Canada has ratified do not automatically become part of the domestic law of Canada so as to enable individuals to go to court when they are breached. Nevertheless, cases may arise regarding domestic law "particularly the Canadian Charter of Rights and Freedoms and federal/provincial/territorial human rights legislation" that are relevant to the implementation of the rights guaranteed by these conventions.

Furthermore, the Supreme Court of Canada has emphasized the importance of taking into account Canada's international obligations in interpreting and applying the Canadian Charter of Rights and Freedoms, both in terms of determining the scope of protected rights and freedoms, and in deciding whether limits on them are acceptable in terms of section 1 of the Charter. This interpretative approach has played a significant role in Charter decisions, and in assisting in the implementation of international human rights treaties.

The position that adherence to international human rights norms is important for the development of domestic law and the realization of social, economic and cultural participation, was stated most eloquently by United Nations High Commissioner for Human Rights, Louise Arbour, when she stated:

> International and national level jurisprudence also helps us to better understand the substantive content of economic, social and cultural rights, and the limits of entitlements and obligations arising there under. *With the international standards and experience in view, it is impossible to regard socioeconomic rights obligations as fanciful or far-fetched.* [Emphasis added.] Human rights of all kinds involve "freedoms" as well as "entitlements." [...] Human rights law insists on principle, rationality and equity in the

process of resource allocation, and on moving steadily forward within the prevailing resource constraints. While the standard of achievement for all countries is the same, the national benchmarks will differ greatly. However, whatever the resource constraints, *there is a core minimum international legal obligation to secure a floor of rights and services beneath which people should never be allowed to fall.* [Emphasis added.][24]

It is critically important for courts to bring their interpretations of domestic legislation into conformity with Canada's international human rights obligations.

Application of International Legal Norms

The United Nations Committee on Economic, Social and Cultural Rights establishes the following test for a member state to meet its obligations under the Covenant on Economic, Social, and Cultural Rights [Covenant] with regard to persons with a disability. The State must:

1. Do much more than merely abstain from taking measures which might have a negative impact on persons with disabilities;

2. Take positive action to reduce structural disadvantages and to give appropriate preferential treatment to people with disabilities in order to achieve the objectives of full participation and equality within society for all persons with disabilities;

3. Employ additional resources for this purpose; and

4. Provide a wide range of specially tailored measures.

VIA Rail failed to meet any portion of the above test for adherence to Canada's obligations under the Covenant. It not only refused to act to accommodate disabled passengers, it has made a conscious effort to purchase inaccessible rail cars. It has failed to provide structural changes, resources or specially tailored measures to remedy the situation. Instead, it has been purposeful in its efforts to purchase and maintain a fleet of rail cars that now are not accessible to the disabled.

---

24. LaFontaine-Baldwin Lecture 2005, "Freedom From Want: From Charity to Entitlement," by Louise Arbour, United Nations High Commissioner for Human Rights.

The Committee sees accessible transportation as directly linked to obligations under Articles 6 to 8—rights relating to work—under the Covenant, and the Standard Rules on the Equalization of Opportunities for Persons with Disabilities. As it stated:

> According to the Standard Rules, persons with disabilities, whether in rural or urban areas, must have equal opportunities for productive and gainful employment in the labour market. For this to happen it is particularly important that artificial barriers to integration in general, and to employment in particular, be removed. As the International Labour Organization has noted, it is very often the physical barriers that society has erected in areas such as transport, housing and the workplace that are then cited as the reason why persons with disabilities cannot be employed. For example, as long as workplaces are designed and built in ways that make them inaccessible to wheelchairs, employers will be able to "justify" their failure to employ wheelchair users.

Similarly, the failure of Governments to ensure that modes of transportation are accessible to persons with disabilities greatly reduces the chances of such persons finding suitable, integrated jobs, taking advantage of educational and vocational training, or commuting to facilities of all types. Indeed, the provision of access to appropriate and, where necessary, specially tailored forms of transportation, is crucial to the realization by persons with disabilities of virtually all the rights recognized in the Covenant.

Under the above interpretation of the Committee, and the concomitant impact of Canada's broad international commitment to accessibility and inclusiveness, the actions taken by VIA Rail may be considered part of systemic barriers that will continue to marginalize, prevent adequate levels of employment, education, and social participation, and diminish the inherent dignity of persons with a disability. Therefore VIA Rail is in breach of a variety of obligations, including Article 11 of the Covenant—the right to an adequate standard of living, as well as Article 12 (right to health), Articles 13 and 14 (right to education), and Articles 12 (liberty of movement) and 25 (political participation) of the Covenant on Civil and Political Rights. The FCA's decision is not reflective of the most recent thinking of the international community regarding the human rights of persons with a disability, and considering Canada's extensive involvement in the drafting of the new convention, I hope the Supreme Court of Canada in making its decision with respect to *CCD v. VIA Rail* Canada looks to the ICRPD for guidance regarding Canada's international human rights commitments.

As well as containing strong provisions promoting equality and opposing disability-based discrimination in draft Article 5 (including through the provision of disability accommodations), the ICRPD also contains extensive provisions on accessibility in draft Article 9. These provisions require the taking of measures to identify and eliminate obstacles and barriers to accessibility, including in the area of transportation, with a view to enabling "persons with disabilities to live independently and participate fully in all aspects of life." Along with the equality and non-discrimination provisions of Article 5, Article 9 of the draft ICRPD is included in that section of the convention having general applicability to all other articles in the convention. This approach is consistent with that outlined by the Committee on Economic, Social and Cultural Rights, and is indicative of the critical role the international community believes accessible transportation plays in the enjoyment of all other human rights by persons with a disability, including the rights to work and employment, health, education, adequate standard of living, independent living, liberty of movement, culture, sport and recreation, access to justice, participation in political life—in short, the full range of civil and political, economic, social, and cultural rights.

Taking into consideration the interpretations of international law discussed above, I firmly believe that Via Rail's actions cannot be said to be consistent either with interpretations of existing international human rights law, or emerging interpretations as elaborated in the draft UNCRDPWD, which will soon be adopted by the United Nations. The critical role of transportation in facilitating access to, and enjoyment of, the full panoply of civil, political, economic, social and cultural rights, necessitates Via Rail's provision of disability accommodations and accessible rail transportation if Canada is to be consistent and in compliance with its human rights obligations under international law.

Conclusion

International human rights obligations have a powerful influence on Canadian legislators and the public. This has benefited PWDs, and other communities.

As the UNCRDPWD is being drafted, it is important to understand the level of that influence and the structure and merit of international treaties. With this, disability NGOs can develop strategies to impact the treaty-making process in order to promote disability rights both domestically and internationally. They may also use the progressive nature of international human rights norms to protect disability rights at home or to advance policy and legislative ideas.

Also, Canada could be a leader in the process by promoting standards that are clearly articulated in domestic legislation, and The Supreme Court of Canada. First, Canada is founded upon constitutional principles that create a sophisticated legal framework. That is, the *Canadian Charter of Rights and Freedoms* continues to balance the interplay of individual and group rights that may occasionally be in conflict. The rule of law, security of the person, equality, and the protection of minorities create the cornerstone of a human rights tradition that empowers and gives dignity to everyone within the Canadian mosaic.

Secondly, Canada's laws creating a "duty to accommodate" persons with a disability "up to the point of undue financial hardship" on the part of the service provider and/or employer is a standard that much of the rest of the world community has yet to reach. It is the legal test necessary to putting teeth in the convention tiger. Canadian expertise can advise on its meaning, establish Canada as a leader in disability rights, and demonstrate Canada's sincerity in providing equality for everyone.

While Canada still has far to go at a domestic level to create a fully inclusive society, its experience in the provision, protection, and promotion of human rights can play a critical role in the development of the UNCRDPWD. Canadian legislators and courts have a tradition of taking human rights seriously and providing a thorough analysis to questions of disability rights. With this, a key principle has been non-discrimination by way of a duty to accommodate persons with a disability. It may be a helpful point of departure for a thorough discussion of the many principles and articles to be contained in the UNCRDPWD as it creates a framework for the international advancement of disability rights.

The UN General Assembly will soon consider the convention text for signature to establish a new rights-based convention that could improve the lives of millions of disabled persons. The process of developing, implementing, and monitoring the UNCRDPWD will be crucial in helping form a framework for international cooperation and provide opportunities to assess shortcomings in domestic models of disability law and policy. A new treaty will also provide international legal accountability regarding disability rights and act as an authoritative universal reference point for domestic law and policy initiatives. It will clarify the content of human rights principles and their application to people with disabilities, provide more effective monitoring mechanisms, and raise awareness about the human rights of people with disabilities.

Finally, by drawing long-awaited public attention to their issues, it could offer capacity-building opportunities for disability groups. However, for the envisioned convention to be truly effective, a good-faith effort at collaboration between member states and NGOs is crucial. According to the UN Standard Rules on the Equalization of Opportunities for People with Disabilities, PWDs have the right to participate in decision making that will ultimately affect their human rights. The process of putting flesh on the bones of a new international human rights instrument must include PWDs on all levels of decision making and at all stages of the process; only in that way can the new treaty truly represent the aspirations and experience of the people it seeks to protect.

By means of the potential of this convention, current states of exclusion and subordination can be transcended and autonomy and self-determination restored to the disabled. Perhaps the convention will meet the objective of the American President John Fitzgerald Kennedy when he said: "I believe in human dignity as the source of international purpose, human liberty as the source of international action, the human heart as the source of national compassion, and the human mind as the source of our invention and our ideas." Stirring words, monumental ideas, definitely relevant to the lives persons with disabilities face in the 21st century and beyond.

Epilogue

From every mountainside let freedom ring...
Martin Luther King

AT THE TIME OF THIS WRITING, I am on the precipice of living in Canada with a significant disability for twenty-five years. With eighteen years on the side of being able-bodied, I have often thought of whether there is a divide. There is no divide because dignity is the essence of all members of the human family.

The great challenge is to establish dignity as inherent to both human form and human action. All too frequently the systems we create exclude, diminish, bar equality, or diminish freedom. I am happy to state that these systems are not irrevocable. They change, they erode, and human will can and does replace gaps in previous norms with renewed vision based on one's potential. This is achieved through a multi-faceted effort that incorporates the Six Degrees of Dignity.

The effort, however, requires tenacity and, above all, courage. Courage to re-enter one's community when after a long period of isolation due to a newly acquired disability, the greatest barrier is fear of not being welcome because disability has caused an overwhelming sense of being diminished by difference of physicality. Courage to trust that a prospective employee or colleague will achieve work standards on an equal basis, although one has not previously been integrated with persons with a disability through school, work or social activity.

Take the dare, be brave, challenge self-doubt, change public perception, improve community support systems, press the envelope of equality laws, demand that legislators develop meaningful policies, and dream. Dream of a better future. Dream of a better future, and believe that it is shared by hundreds of millions of other souls across the globe.

In leaving these final remarks, I have been reminded of the kindness of my sister Jan, when she recorded a cassette tape with many of the Beatles hits for me to listen to when I was hospitalized after my injury. This is of critical value when held in bed completely immobilized. Several times I replayed both "Yesterday" and "The Long and Winding Road." With support, yesterday was not the miserable state of emotional paralysis described by Paul McCartney, it was the day before today. The road to community participation would be long, and even after twenty-five years it continues to wind, create uphill battles, and be torn by extreme weather, but it does come back to the door of dignity and freedom.

I am happy to state that the past quarter century has seen progress for persons with a disability, traditionally marginalized groups, and all Canadians. From that simple word "equality" has arisen great emotions and concerted effort among the disability community. Through progressive programs, policy, social, individual, and judicial development, "equality" has evolved from a statement in the constitution to a guarantee that a person with a disability does not merely have a right to equal opportunity before the law. Today, if they face discrimination they must be given substantive equality where the disability is accommodated up to the point of undue financial hardship.

In the future, achieving "equality" must also be more than a positive statement or a bean-counting exercise in undue hardship. If economic, social, and cultural rights are not given to persons with the disability in a meaningful way then dignity, development, and equality cannot be fully achieved. Persons with a disability must be lifted out of poverty to realize personal security. They must know the dignity of a job and participation in the community in order to break the bonds of discrimination. They must feel comfortable in their self-expression and artistic development to know that their contribution to this great country is truly appreciated. It is through achieving the Six Degrees of Dignity in a consistently holistic fashion that human rights will prevail to improve the lives of persons with a disability and create a better Canada.

And so the song continues…

I have walked that long road to freedom. I have tried not to falter; I have made missteps along the way. But I have discovered the secret that after climbing a great hill, one only finds that there are many more hills to climb. I have taken a moment here to rest, to steal a view of the glorious vista that surrounds me, to look back on the distance I have come. But I can rest only for a moment, for with freedom comes responsibilities, and I dare not linger, for my long walk is not yet ended.

Nelson Mandela

About the Author

As a person with quadriplegia, the result of spinal cord injury at the age of 18, **David Shannon** has used a wheelchair for the past 25 years. During this time, he has been committed to policy development and legal advocacy for the protection of human rights and community integration for persons with a disability.

David received his undergraduate degree from Lakehead University in Thunder Bay and law degree from Dalhousie University in Halifax. He later attended the London School of Economics and Political Science for his LL.M. studies, where he focused on the advancement of second-generation human rights norms.

In 1997, at the age of 34, David took his wheelchair 9,000 kilometres across Canada to promote empowerment for disenfranchised communities and greater social inclusion for all Canadians. David Shannon's Cross Canada Tour took two years to plan, 197 days to complete, and involved 5,000 volunteers and participants. During the tour, David wheeled for 10-hour days and spoke directly to 20,000 people.

David is the recipient of many awards and honours, including the Queen's Jubilee Medal for his commitment to human rights and community service. He was the founding chair of the Accessibility Advisory Council of Ontario, and a member of the Ontario Human Rights Tribunal. He continues to sit on numerous boards and committees, among them, the Canadian Association of Independent Living Centres, the Council of Canadians with Disabilities, and the Tetra Society of Ontario.

The Shannon Law office, located in Thunder Bay, Ontario, practices primarily in administrative law and civil litigation. David's advocacy and academic interests have centred on civil rights mechanisms that promote freedoms for persons who face medico-legal forms of incarceration, and do not have community-based supports.

In August of 2006, David represented the Canadian Association of Independent Living Centres in meetings of the United Nations ad hoc committee to draft a comprehensive *Convention on the Rights and Dignity of Persons With a Disability*. The Convention was adopted by all member states, and will be before the United Nations General Assembly in fall 2006 for signature and ratification.

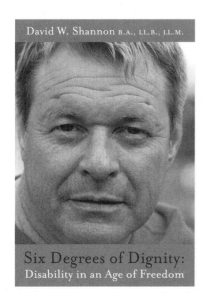

David W. Shannon B.A., LL.B., LL.M.

Six Degrees of Dignity:
Disability in an Age of Freedom

To order copies of

Six Degrees of Dignity:
Disability in an Age of Freedom

by David W. Shannon

Contact
Creative International Bound Inc.
at 613-831-7628 (Ottawa)
or 1-800-287-8610
(toll-free in North America)

Or order online at
www.creativebound.com

To inquire about our discounts for wholesale, retail, library, educational, association, or multiple-copy orders, please call us at 1-800-287-8610 or email us at orderdesk@creativebound.com.

Six Degrees of Dignity by David Shannon is available in bookstores across Canada.